My Life in Pages

My Life in Pages

A book of poems and short stories

Copyright © 2018 Solaine Gerhard
All rights reserved reproduction of the whole or any parts of the contents without written permission is prohibited.

Written and Illustrated by Solaine Gerhard

Edited by Sophia Pisana

ISBN-10: 1986693678
ISBN-13: 978-198663677

Acknowledgements

To those who have invoked on my emotions.

Table of Contents

My Life in Pages 1

Who am I? 3

I am... 4

Who are you? 6

Inversion of Perception 8

Their Lives Matter 10

Time 13

Confliction 15

Temptation of Bright Blue Eyes 17

Anger VS Strength 19

Defeated 21

Have Mercy... On Me 22

Lucky in Space 25

Internal 27

Destruction by Words 29

The Girl Down the Street 30

Rebirth 32

The Rainbow 34

One in the Same 36

The Noise of Doubt 38

Mary Jane, Molly and Margarita 40

A Distraction 42

Becoming the Card Dealer 44

Downing in Tears 46

Dabhan (Devin) 48

All I Know	50
Disappointment	52
Reaper	54
Head Held High	56
Forever	58
A Kiss to Bind Us	60
Color Drip	62
Touching Bodies	64
Snake in the Garden	66
Rise	68
Unwritten Love	70
Alone	72
Nonsense	75
Pinky Promise	77
Smoke	79
Transfer of Pain	81
A Reason to Live	83
A Zephyr	85
Howls of the Lone Wolf	86
Eyes	89
Dying Kiss	91
Actions	92
Find Yourself	96
Alcoholic Reasons	98
Beauty of Words	100
View	102
I Am Not Yours	105

Their Voices	106
S.A.D. and Company	109
I Wonder	110
Trust	112
Me Too	114
Pit of my Stomach	117
Everyday	118
Suicide	120
The Grin Reaper	122
I Am My Own Motivation	124
Desire	126
Taylor	129
He Saved Her	131
Abandoned	137
The City of the Rich	139

My Life in Pages

My life can be written,

In pages,

For you to read.

My life can be written,

In simplicity,

Or full of metaphors.

My life is worth more than these words,

But for now,

These words,

Are all that I have.

Who am I?

Who am I?
Who am I to be called different?
Who am I to be called the same?
Who am I to be judged upon appearance?
My voice, my skin, my culture?
Am I not a human, just like you.

I am…

I am an anxiety ridden ticking bomb, walking down the streets ready to explode.
Or rather implode on myself.

I am panic at the front door, waiting for what lies beyond the broken wooden frame.
My thoughts are odd, dark and twisted.

I am fear of the unknown, prediction is a safe haven I don't have the pleasure of knowing.
What is my destiny?

I am disappointment of the truth, hard to take in but none the less reality.
Lies are an ignorant bliss.

I am the shattered image, broken hearted and full with tears.
Heavy is the soul that weeps.

I am the deepest weakness, the secrets locked away in the bottom of the chest.
Don't let them out.

I am quite alone, metaphorically speaking within the depths of my own mind.
The emptiness is where I hide.

I am: Screaming Out Loud, Angry, Inching Near Envy

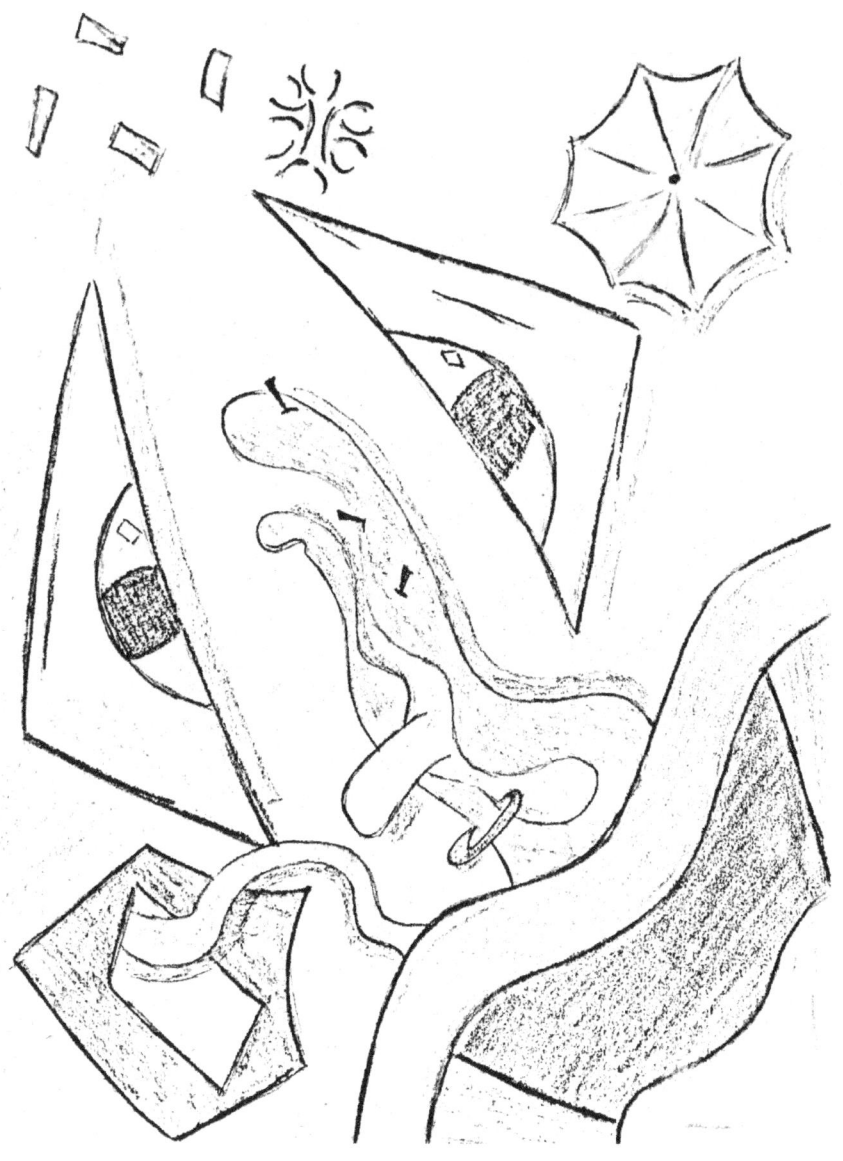

Who are you?

Who are you but the nightmares to my dreams?
What is your purpose?
To show me the life of the short lived?
I hear nothing but the deafened cries of the dead
Leave my mind and let me be
The thoughts you bring burden my days
An impersonating fire that frightens me
Tossed in a salad of emotions
Only to be left with watery eyes
Lift your image
And haunt me no more.

Inversion of Perception

Cold winds sting upon my face
Holding onto you a warm embrace

Tall green trees sway in sync
Their leaves fall off link by link

Clouds of gray, shape into whatever your imagination may please
But if I look up into the sky would it become the sea?

The sea below the sky above
Flying high and low a snow-white dove

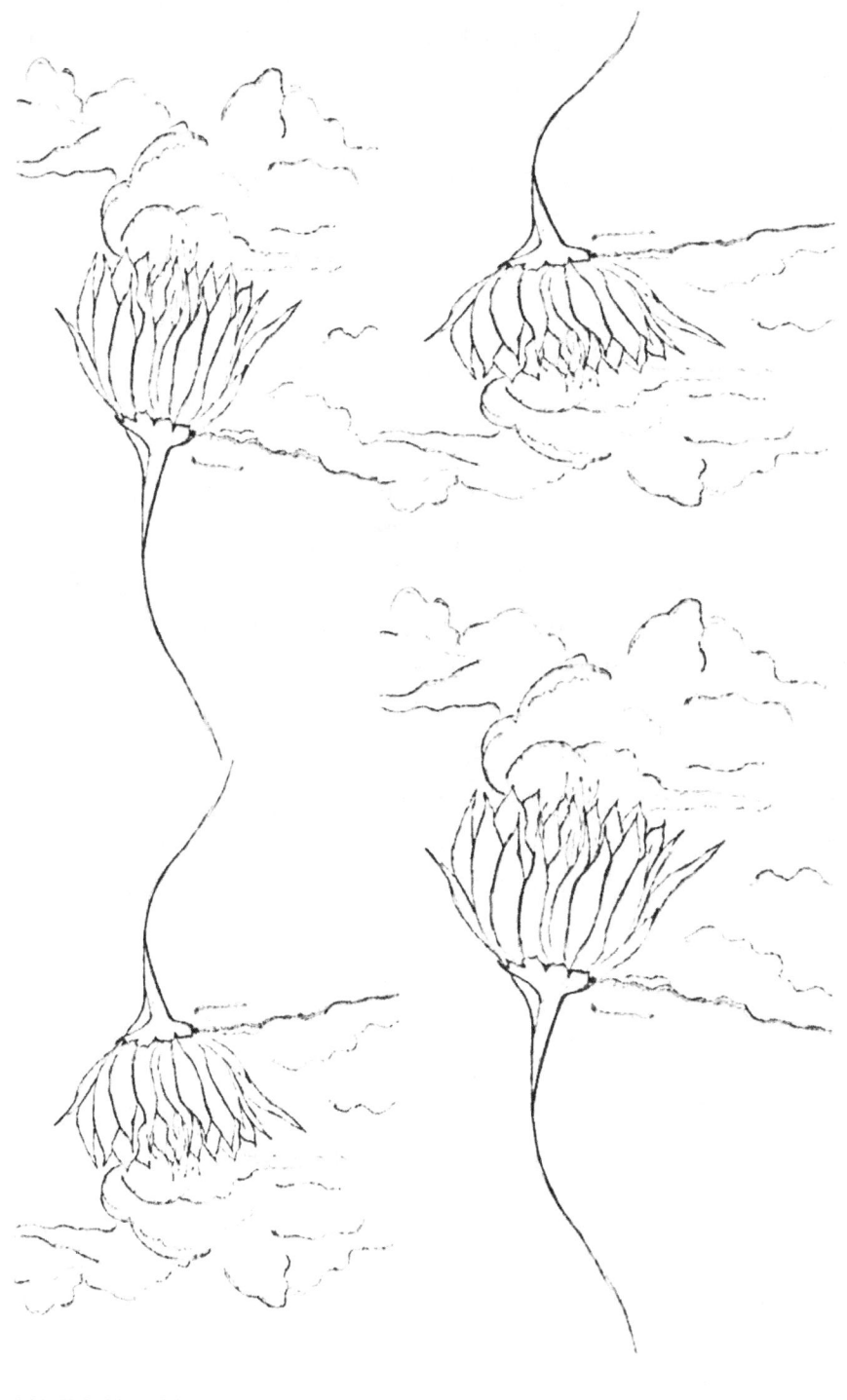

Their Lives Matter

Wondering, thinking, a memory
Nodding, shaking, do they agree

Their eyes are wide
They've lost all pride

For what was known
Is now overthrown

They sweat in heat
For if not their beat

Bandanas worn across thy head
New day comes o' they dread

Work in fields of corn and cotton
Faith and God is all they've gotten.

Time

Stuck between the past
Afraid to venture into the future
My life cannot be held back
But I cannot move on
No time with me
My hour glass empty

Confliction

A struggle between my real and spiritual body.

Can you love me?
Respect me?
And protect me?

The pain has made me suffer.
The knowledge that you can never be mine has left my heart broken.

Though the days go on.
My heart is left unhealed.

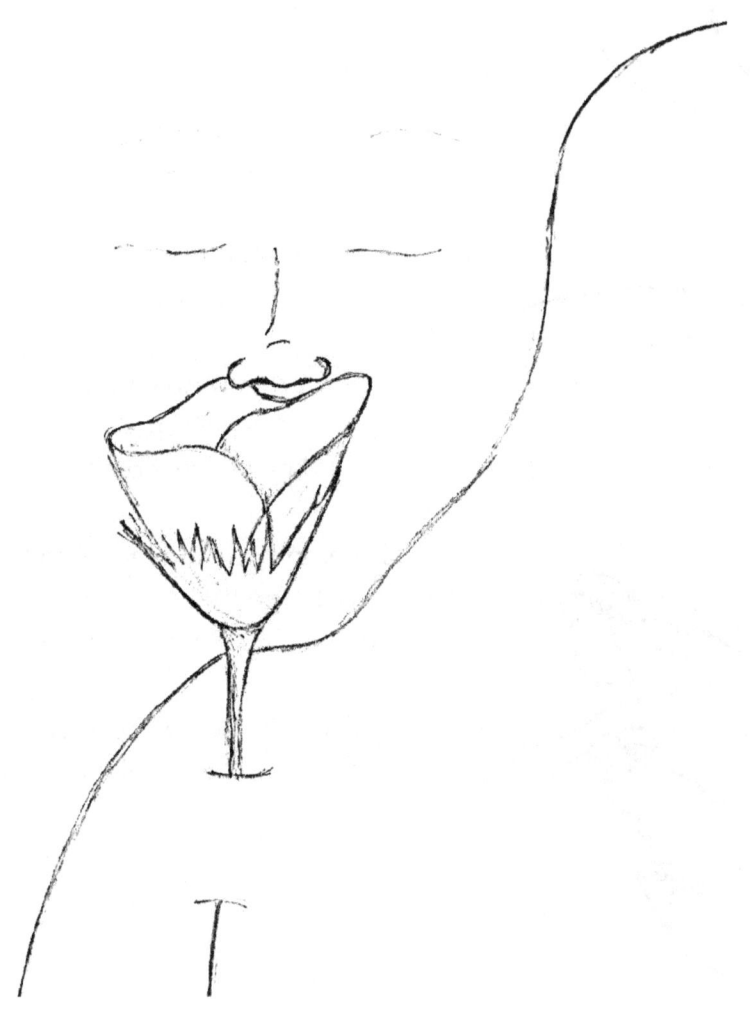

Temptation of Bright Blue Eyes

Tempting as you are
Staring me down
Soothing, yet seductive ocean eyes
Radiant, you light up my world
The sun has an opponent
And that would be you
Your presence excites me
Hearts racing, blood pumping
I'm addicted to your ways
Leave me speechless with the way you look at me
Kiss me and make me forget
Hypnotize me so all I know is you.

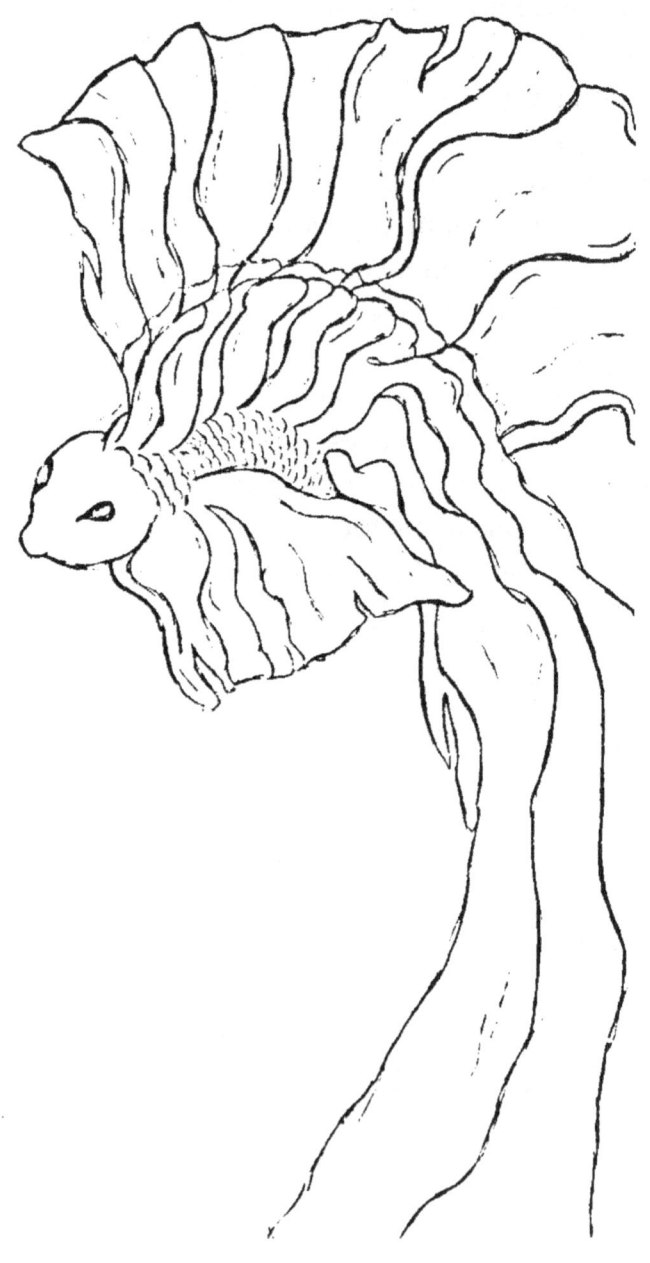

Anger VS Strength

The anger has taken over
My body under a spell
I feel no pain
Only the hot tears as they fall down my cheeks
I bite my lips and taste the blood
Run harder, faster, longer
Every pound, every time I touch the ground
Shocks to my knees
The inevitable pain of grinding bones
Pulse raising
100, 120, 180
Wheezing, finding breathing difficult
Still I continue
Weak to others
But if this doesn't kill me
Strength with triumph

Defeated

Misplaced, misunderstood
Smart, but not bright
Walks around with a frown upon her face
She should smile more they say
"Let's see those pearly whites"
But no joy comes to her
Too stressed about nothing
These situations that should not affect her
Her heart is too big, but not too strong

Have Mercy… On Me

Show me the way
Show me the way to a greater me
The way to things that men never thought possible
The possibilities to do
The power to get it done

Show me the way to strength
The strength not to hold more than one-thousand elephants
But the strength to trust
The strength to love
The strength to forgive

Shine your light upon me
Remove the dark clouds that block my view
Let loose the birds that sing and praise
Shine upon me your light
Shine upon me the knowledge to do and create

Allow me to do so
Allow me to see the path
The path lit up by your greatness
Allow me to walk upon your path
To gaze upon the magnificent view shown to me

Save me
Save me from this person who does no good
This person whose decisions make me weary
Save me from the evil I see
From the anger and the sadness

Save me…
Save me from myself

Cleanse my soul
Cleanse my body
Cleanse me for I have sinned

I have done wrong upon this world
Upon this day
The days before
And the days to come

I wish to sin no more
For I have sinned upon the land that your son died on
This world in which you created
Sacrificing your son for me and all for mankind
So that we may live

Save me for I want to be with you

Lucky in Space

The stars, the sun,
the moon, the space,
Lost in a galaxy
And I don't want to be found
Hide-and-seek in the milky way
Loving being oh so far away
No stressing
No worrying
Wishing you could join me in my journey through the universe
Swimming in Saturn's rings
Floating in Jupiter's atmosphere
Skipping along the craters
Making wishes on the shooting stars
"I wish"
And wait till the day they come true.

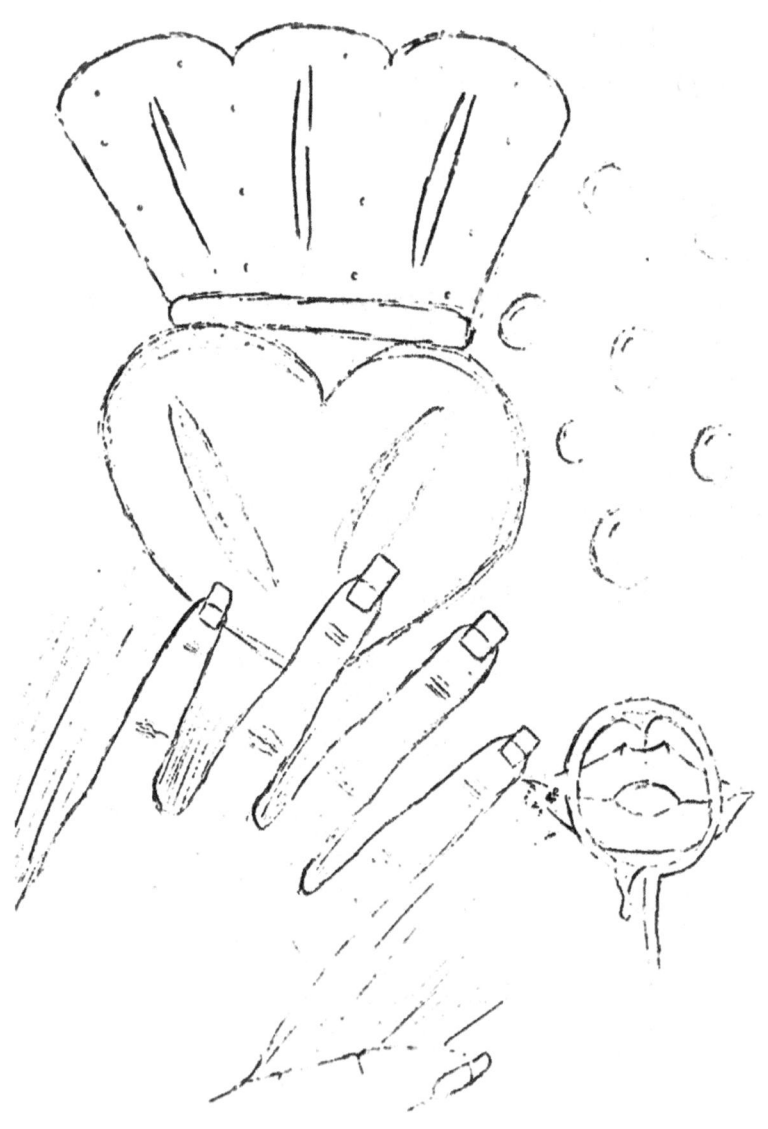

Internal

I'm done with the pain
With the regret and the worries
I've let it rule my world for too long
I'm done pretending to be okay

I'm not.

I'm hurting inside

Slowly eroding from what you've done

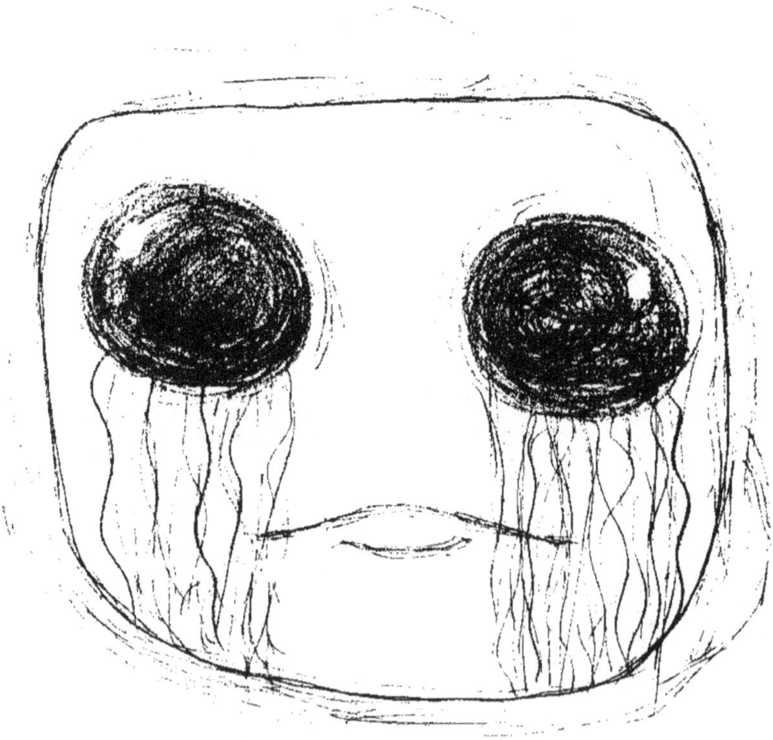

Destruction by Words

The screaming and yelling that destroys everything we've worked for
Between you and them
Them, there is no you
Not anymore
I have no room for you in my heart
No love to give your way
And now he has taken your place
To heal the wounds you've created
To seal this gap that left me gasping for air
To stop the hurt
And end the pain.

The Girl Down the Street

The sullen look on her face
The creases by her mouth give away the years of sorrow
Expressionless, the mellowness of her walk leaves the crowd guessing
What is her story?
She was a girl, alive and strong
Grew up in the world with what she needed
Yet she was naïve
Soon alone in the world
Nothing but the clothes on her back to call her own
Stripped of her innocence
Had her kindness taken from her
The love she had vanished
She was nothing more but a face in the crowd
With no purpose
She only wanted to see the light
Lay down her useless body
And rest in peace.

Rebirth

Get up and move the world,
don't think twice.
Leave your conscience behind,
and travel farther beyond everything else.

Don't let them talk you down,
unleash that person you've been keeping a secret.
Getting rid of all insecurities,
and moving on to living in prosperity.

Deny negativity,
accept positivity.
Access your alter ego,
and the true meaning will come.

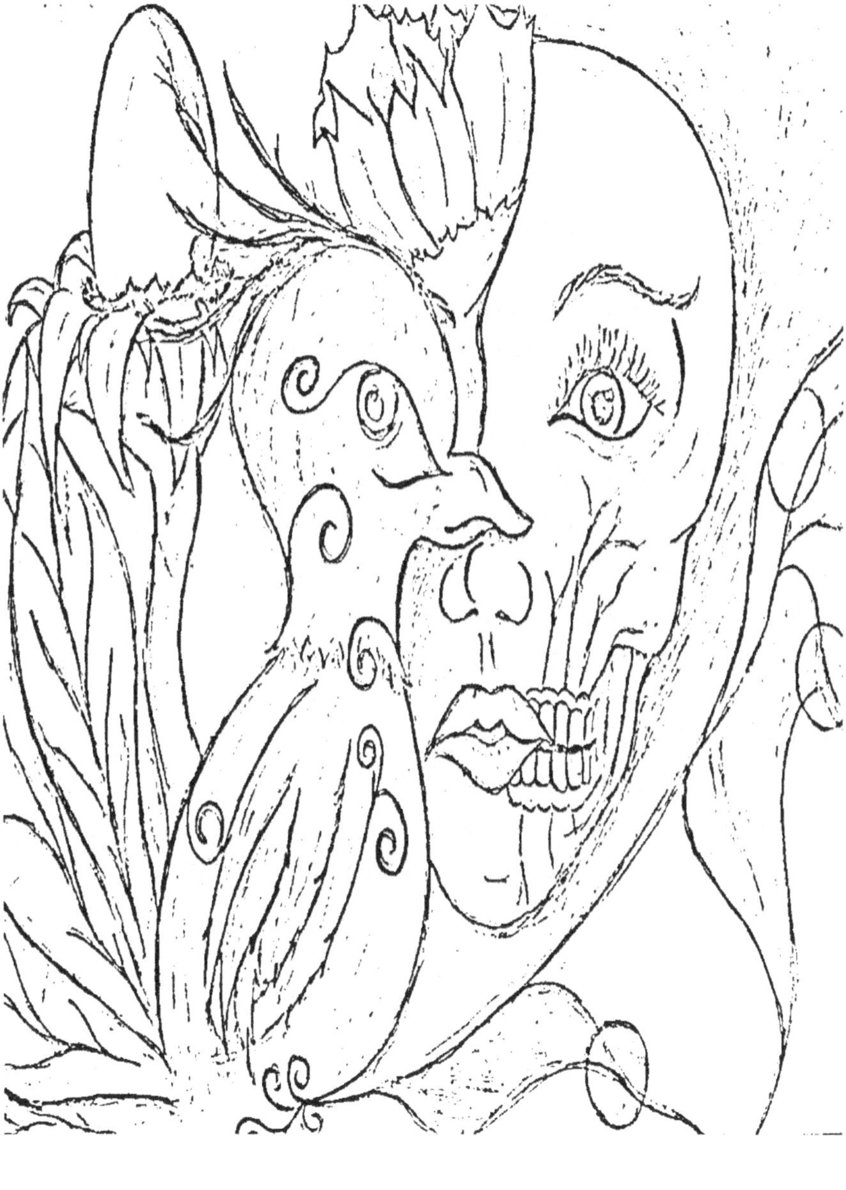

The Rainbow

With or without any doubt
There has been change in my life
Dramatic and emotional
Dreadful and irritating
Soothing and comforting
But mostly just plain change
To be thrown in the path of an emotional tornado
Leaving behind a past of hurt and un-satisfaction
Tearing apart whatever is thrown in its way
A hurricane broils in the horizon
The heavy tears of rain
The erotic strength to knock anything down
The eye of the storm
Calm and relaxed
Reassuring and peaceful
A liar
Realization hits hard
And the pain starts again
Spinning around and around
Dizzy, confused, frustrated, disappointed, alone
The wind picks up and the tears fall again
But at the end of every storm comes something worth while
Life, survival, the rainbow at the end of the storm.

One in the Same

Do we not both use our mouths?

Do you not use your tongue to say those things?

Do I hear differently from what you imply?

If you could not see me and could only hear me, would you have the same image of me?

I am not like you…

but we are not that different.

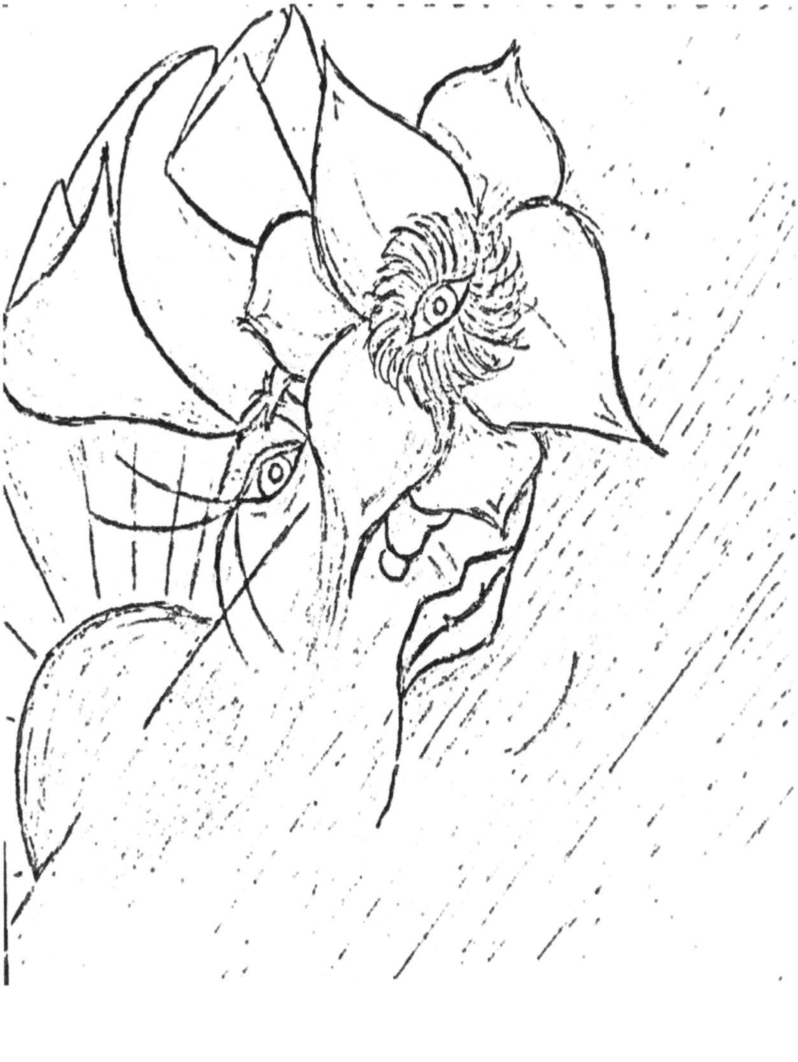

The Noise of Doubt

So many thoughts running through my head
An everlasting insomnia consumes me

Could have
Should have
Would have

No regrets but always worries
These heavy eyes will not shut
With pits and patters through the night

Restless and sleepless
Dwelling in the past
Dueling with the future
Do I even exist?

For this nocturnal state has taken over
Thinking no blinking
My heartaches his mistakes
Rattle snakes and mice fight in my head

These thoughts keep coming through the night
Will I ever close my eyes and see the light?

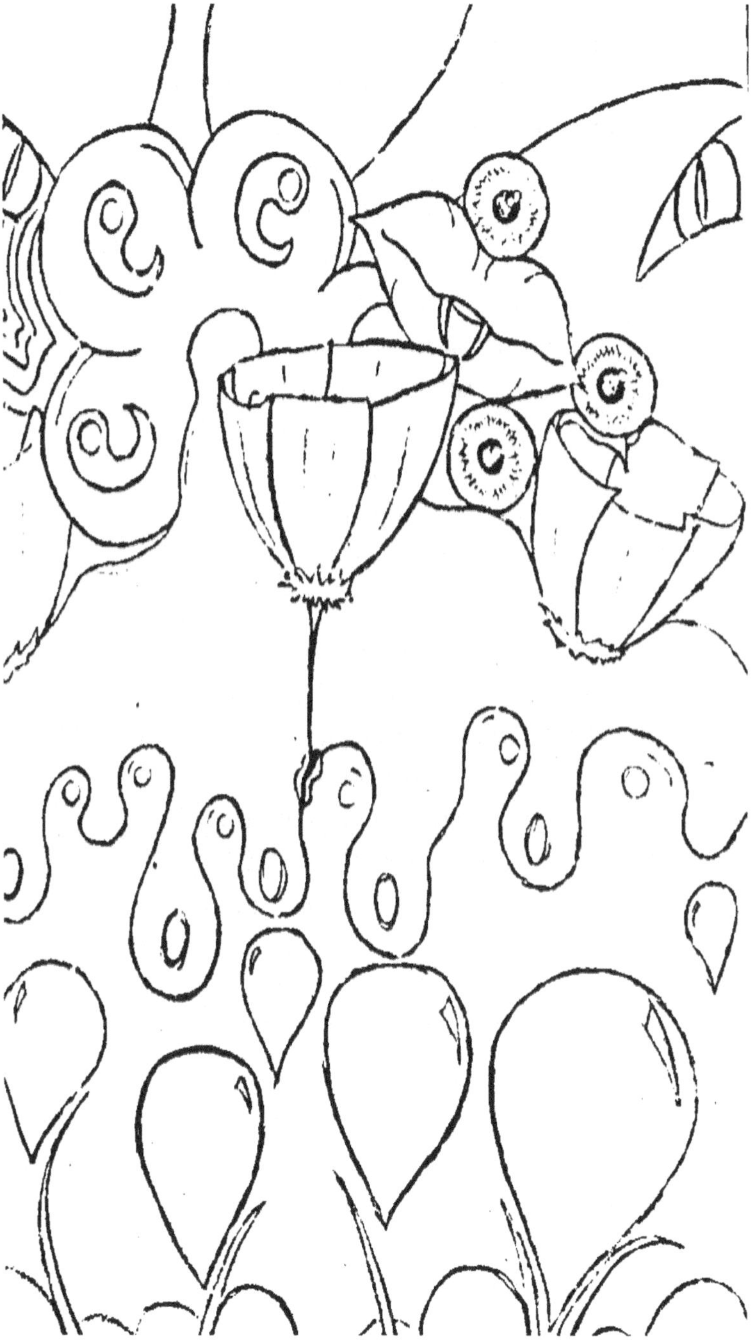

Mary Jane, Molly and Margarita

Temptation meets me at the door
Lingering around my shoulders
Whispering the sins I should commit
Take this lighter
Spark this bowl
Inhale, exhale
Uncap this pill bottle
Pop, then swallow
Lust for water
Trust for better
Pour it
Sip it
Chug it
Savor it
Let the burn take over
Let your inhibition vanish
Open up and never go back down
Watch your step
The comedown is far
Temptation stays a lift
As you fall to your fate

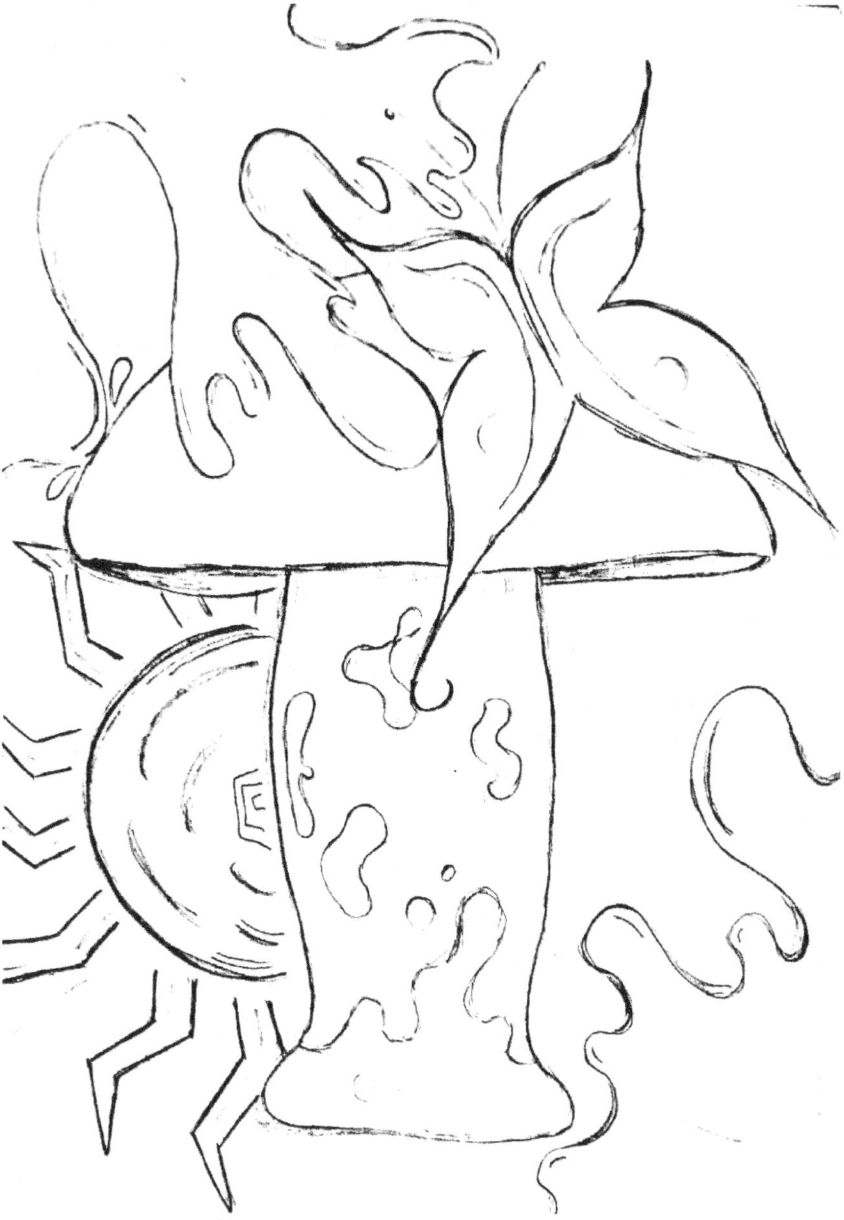

A Distraction

I lay with you at night.
Your arms are around me, but they hug someone else,
The lips you lay upon my back weren't meant for my body.
I can see the thoughts you think, and I'm not the one you think of.

But I lay with you at night.
Embracing everything you put me up to, caressing hands against me.
Trailing along the goose bumps that arise when you say my name.

Say my name, but that is all, I don't want to listen to you speak.
Your words do nothing for me but make me regret everything.

Just kiss me and think of her.
Because I'm thinking of him.

But don't regret me now baby.
You better appreciate me now baby.
Take me as a memory baby.
I know you want to go back baby.

But the wrongs we're committing cannot be undone,
You're my distraction baby,
So lay with me till the sun comes up.

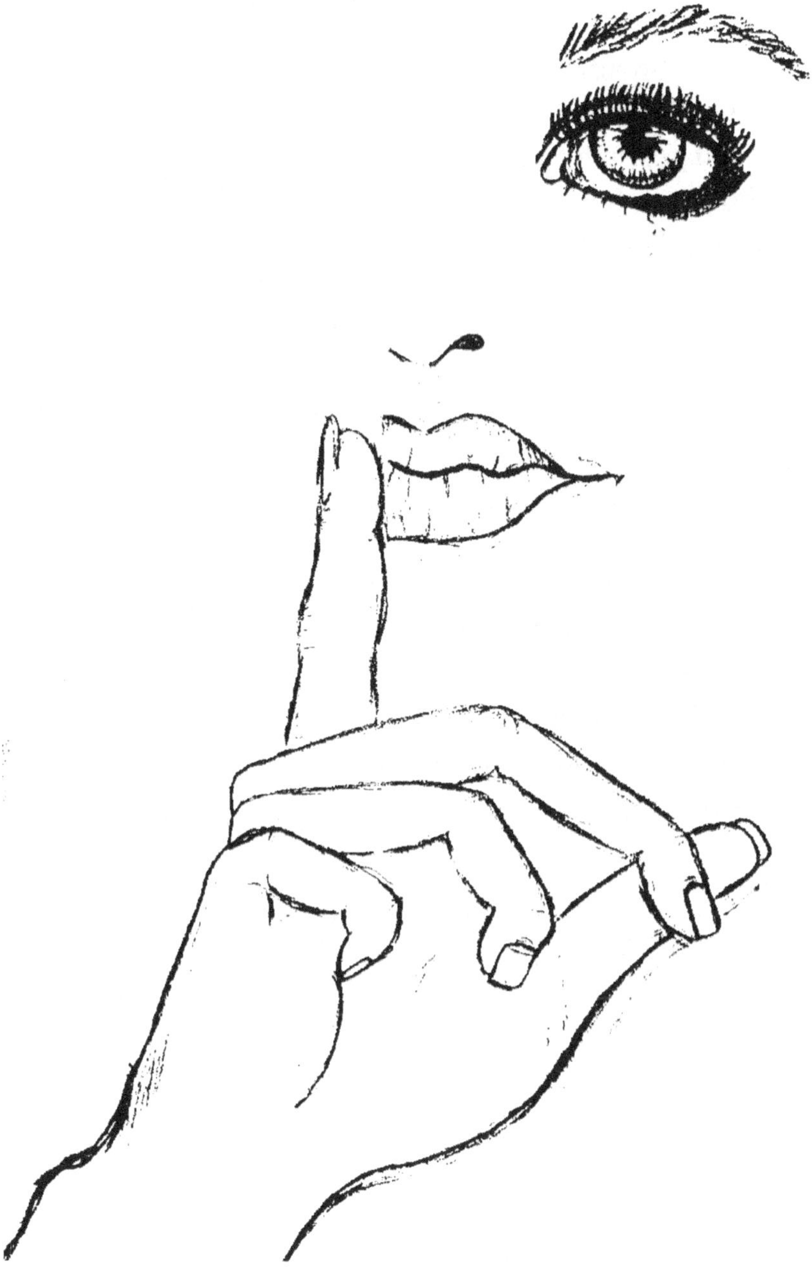

Becoming the Card Dealer

Get past the pain
Take a deep breath
No lies yes, it'll hurt
No lies it'll get better with practice
Don't hold me down
Keep me up to pace
Don't leave me behind
Lay down the cards, I got the ace
It's done
I'm the king
Taking my queen to the head
But no more time for games
No more time for the joker
These rules are to be broken
But when it comes to my heart
That is to be left alone
Yes, its beauty bewilders you
But touch, and its off with your head.

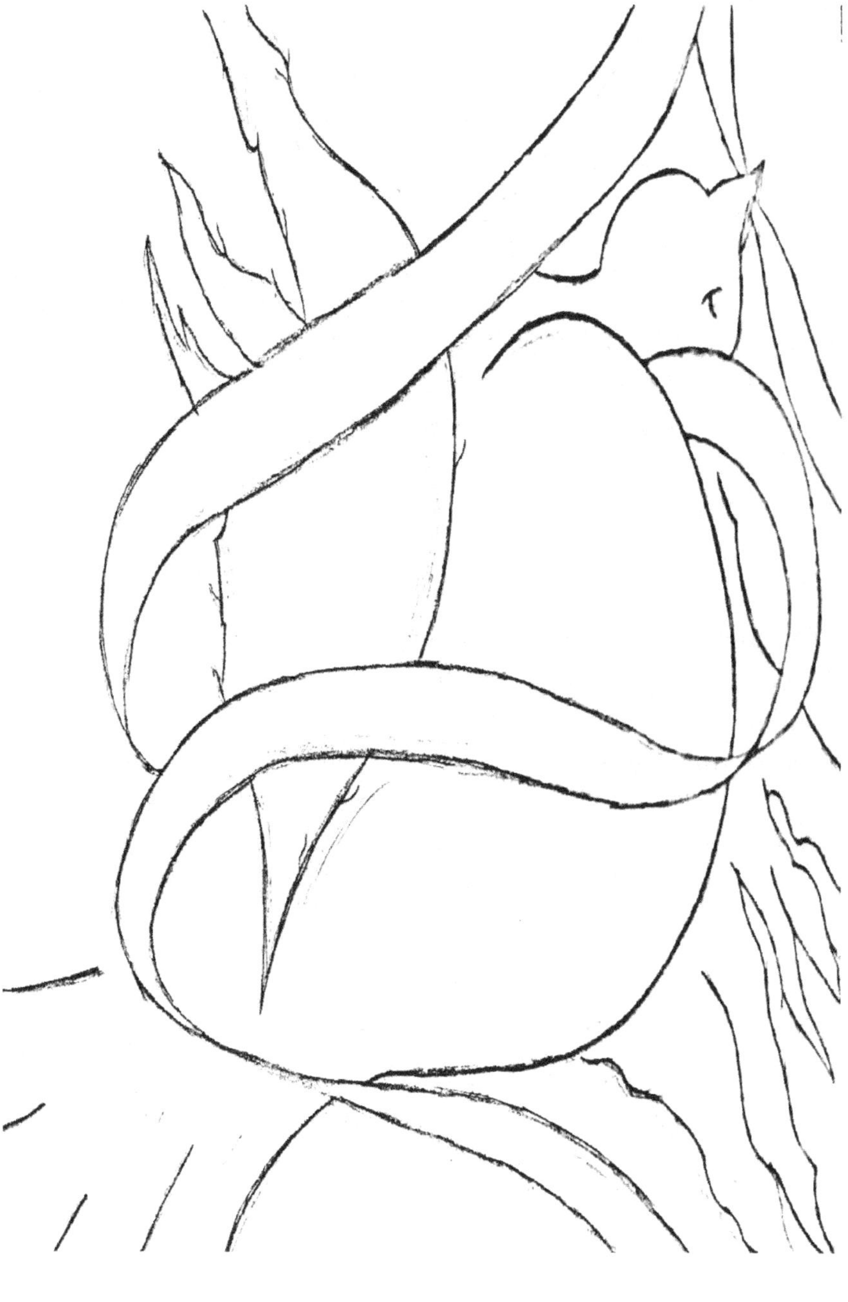

Downing in Tears

These heavy tears fall down my cheeks
The weights that hold me make me weak
The waves of snores I hear ashore
All eroded memories,
they hurt no more.

Keep me now or keep me never
Open hearts don't last forever
Living, thriving, cease to waiting
Familiar faces,
slowly fading.

Voices merge, it's just one now
Thoughts are lucid, I'm dreaming now
Tides are high, don't let me drown
Save me soon,
then lay me down.

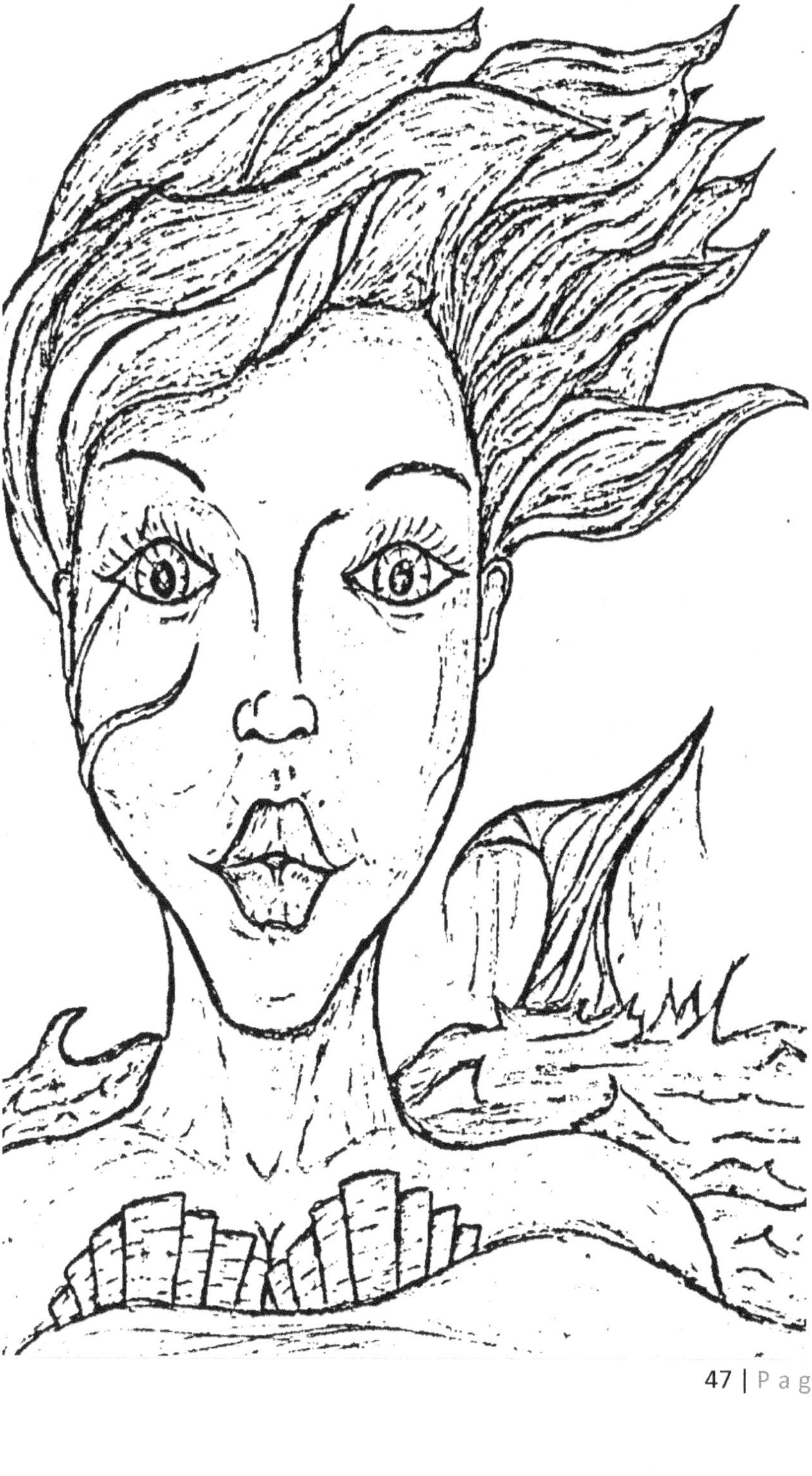

Dabhan (Devin)

Little dark one,
Worthy of praise,
Hold on to the what you have left.

Grasp what you have coming your way,
I won't leave you now.

The companionship you give allows no misery,
Only the opportunity for better.

Relax and unravel those you kept tangled tight,
The world isn't as bad as you think.

Hold my hand, I can help you through it all,
You don't need to be broken anymore.

The pieces are all around you,
Waiting to be assembled.

I have the first, let me place it over your heart,
Take a step forward and the rest will follow.

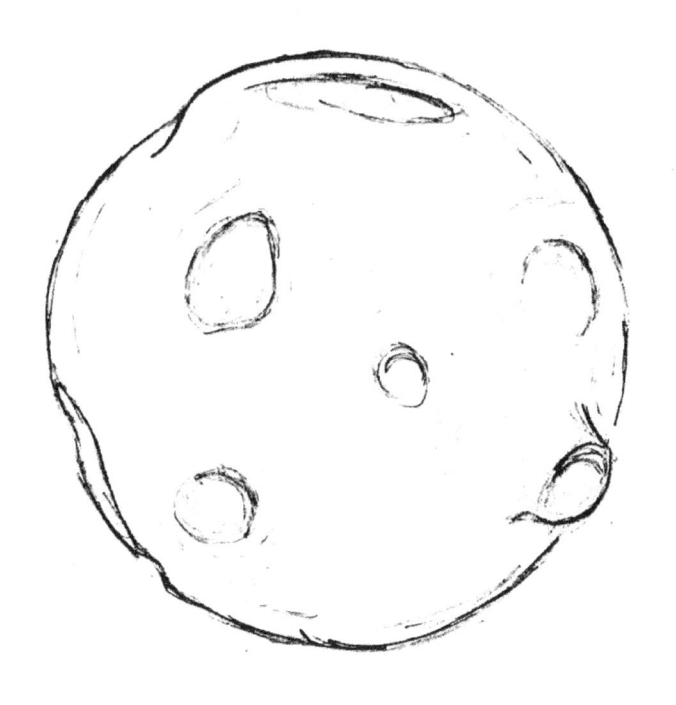

All I Know

All I know are emotions.

All I know are the sullen cries that seep into my pillow.

Do you know what it means?

To be heartbroken?

To feel yourself slowly fade?

Once a rose, now a stem.

All I know,

Is how I feel.

Disappointment

These tears upon my mother's face,
Her daughters she feels full of disgrace.

Leading tempting lives, not so holy,
Bless us father, faith is fading slowly.

Let consequences rise for choices are made,
Things of taboo, our bodies we degrade.

Forgive us, but your children will grow,
A cycle repeats and your pain we will know.

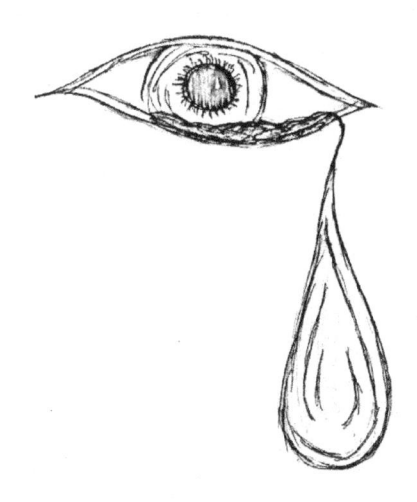

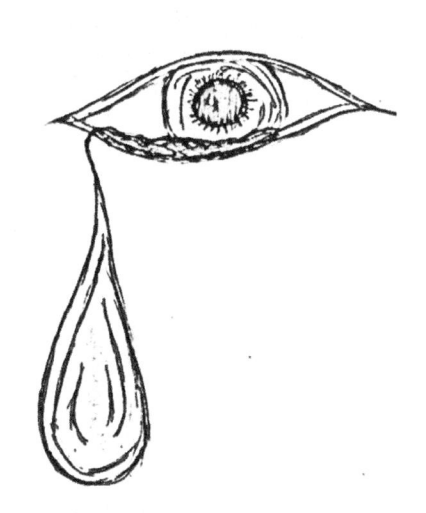

Reaper

Alluring eyes stray deep
No signs of the living here
Death sat in the corner
Waiting for me to enter the room
No lights
No spoken words
A cloak over bones
Dried and un-youthful
They reached out for me
No white horse in sight
Chains wrapped around me
No escape from myself

Head Held High

With inspiration
     and creativity,
          with pride,
              and dignity

I will become all the things you thought I couldn't be.

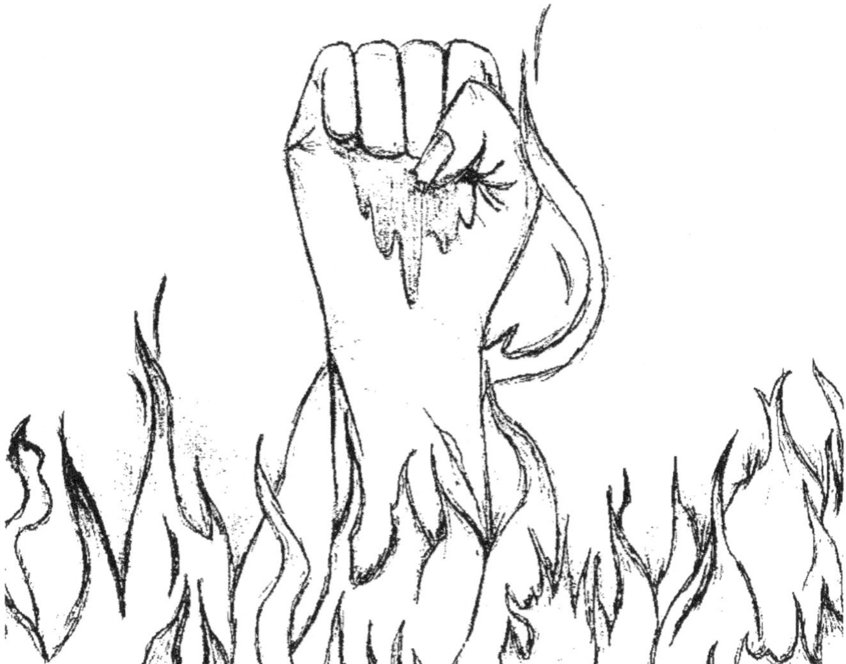

Forever

Do you understand me?
Look into my eyes
Touch me like you mean it
Hold me in your hands
Leave your thoughts at the door
No time for judgments
Here in the moment
Let me be the one
Look into my eyes
And see forever

A Kiss to Bind Us

You're just a kiss away
No one to tell you otherwise
You're just a kiss away
So, what are you waiting for?

New memories we create
The past we left but never forget
Can you see the life in my eyes?
It fades when your touch leaves my skin

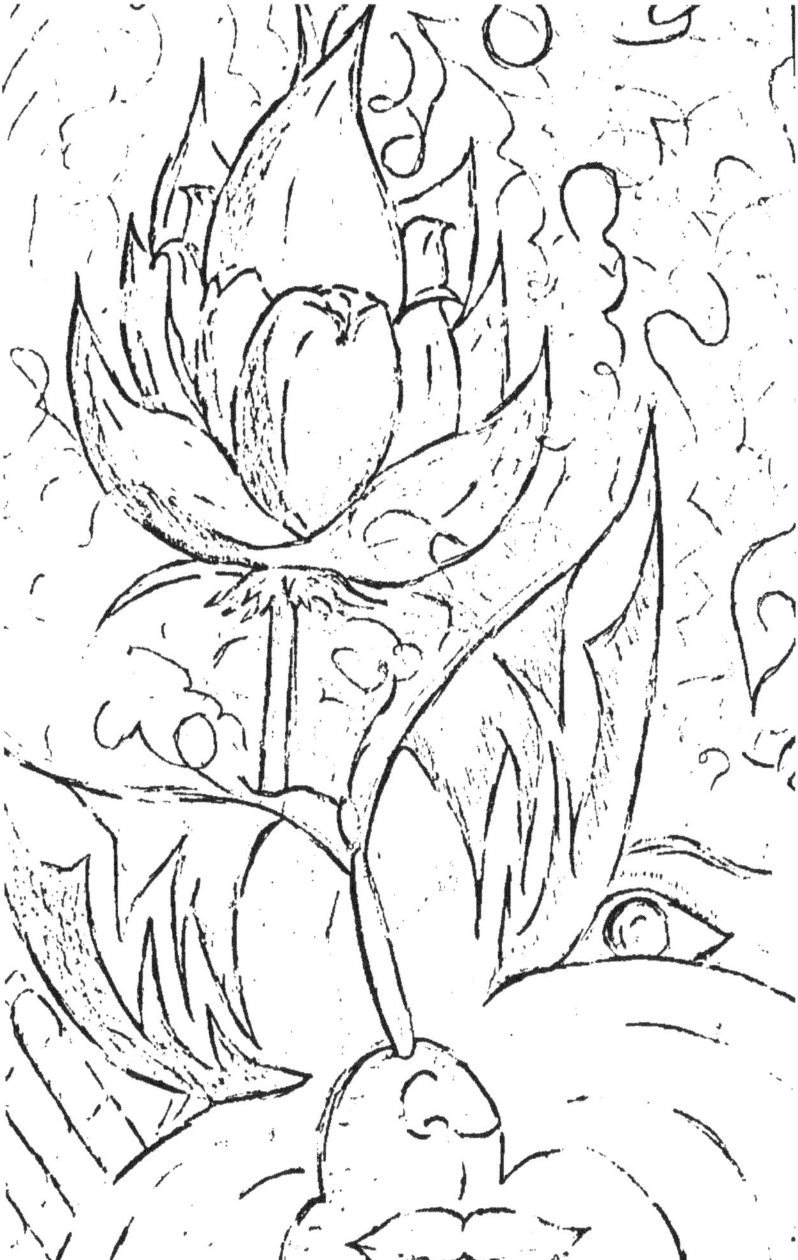

Color Drip

Write my thoughts down.
See the dreams I draw for you.
Let the colors consume you.
Total unconscious control.
Eyes wide open.
As I feed your mind my views.

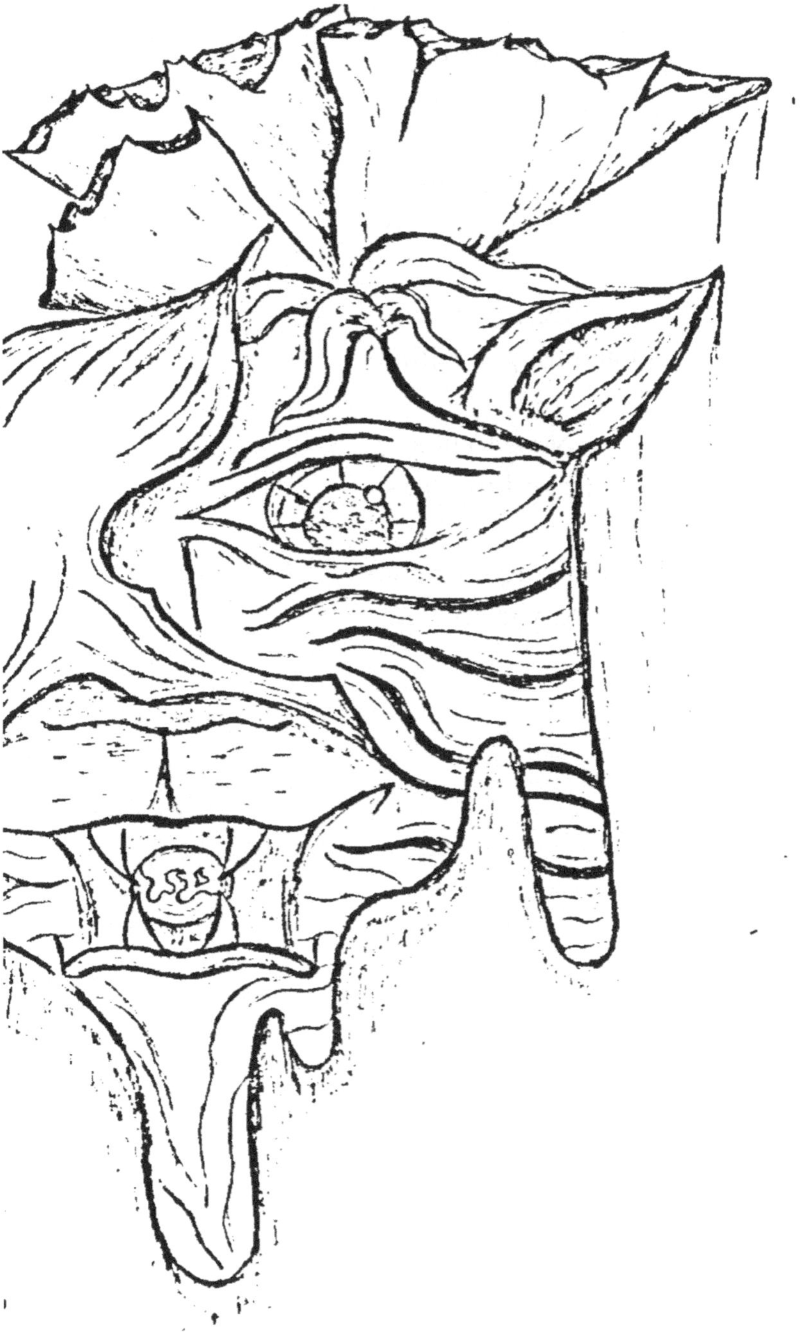

Touching Bodies

Eyes watch eyes
Each with lies.

Lips kiss lips
Each kinetic trips.

Ear for an ear
Each fought with fear.

Nose to nose
Friend thy foes.

Chin against chin
Never give in.

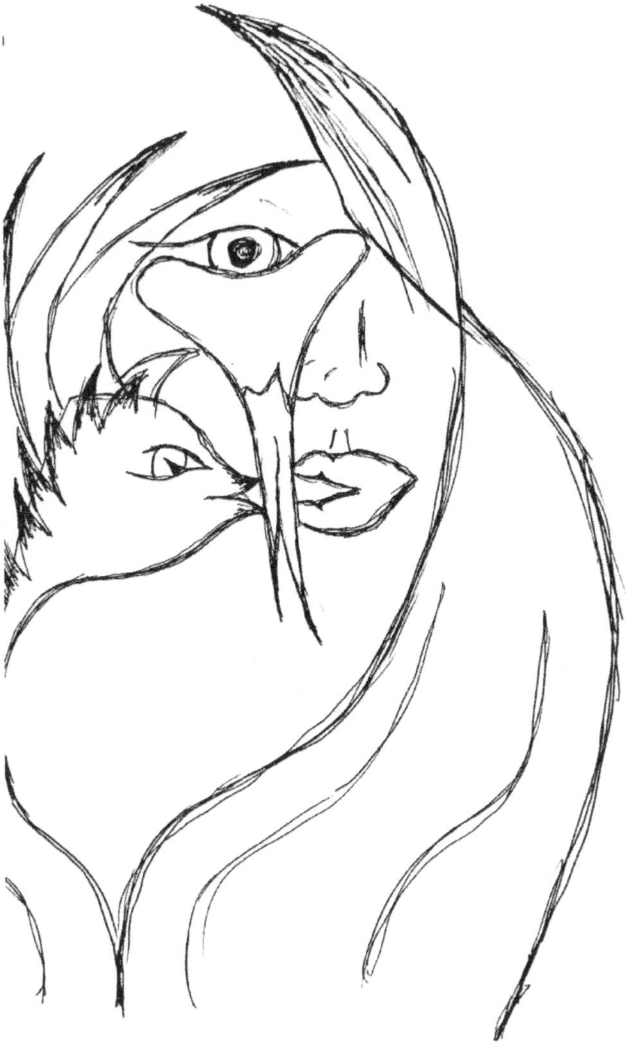

Snake in the Garden

The time is near
Your body is pure
Run from evil
And from the devil
Corruption is upon you
As the grass drips dew
Hold your breath and say a prayer
The time is now and forever.

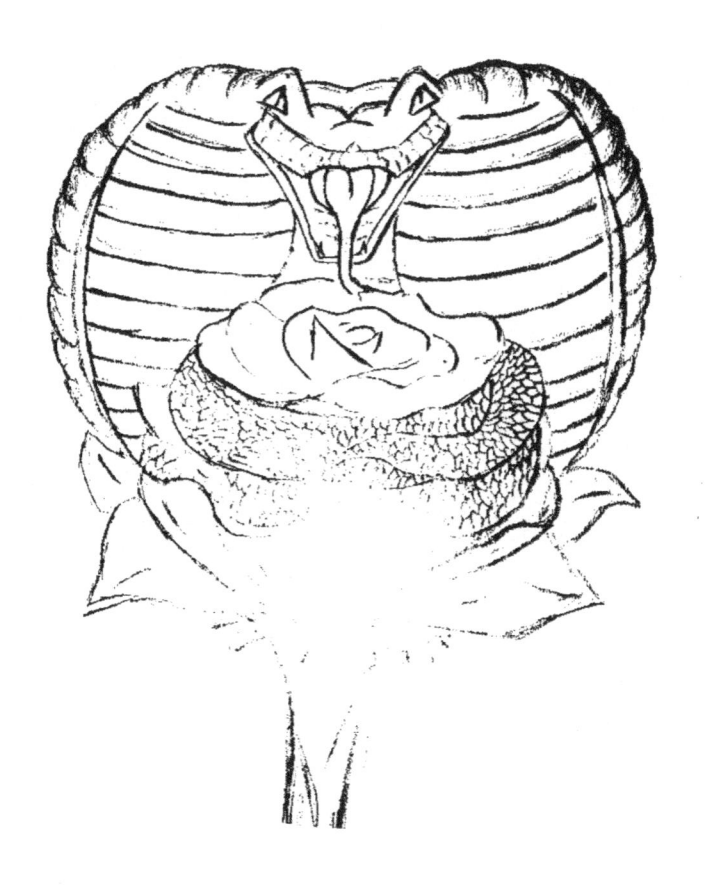

Rise

The sun comes up
The sun goes down
The sun will rise again

I wake up
I go to sleep
I will rise again

The sun is bright and so am I
So, I will shine too

غ ط س

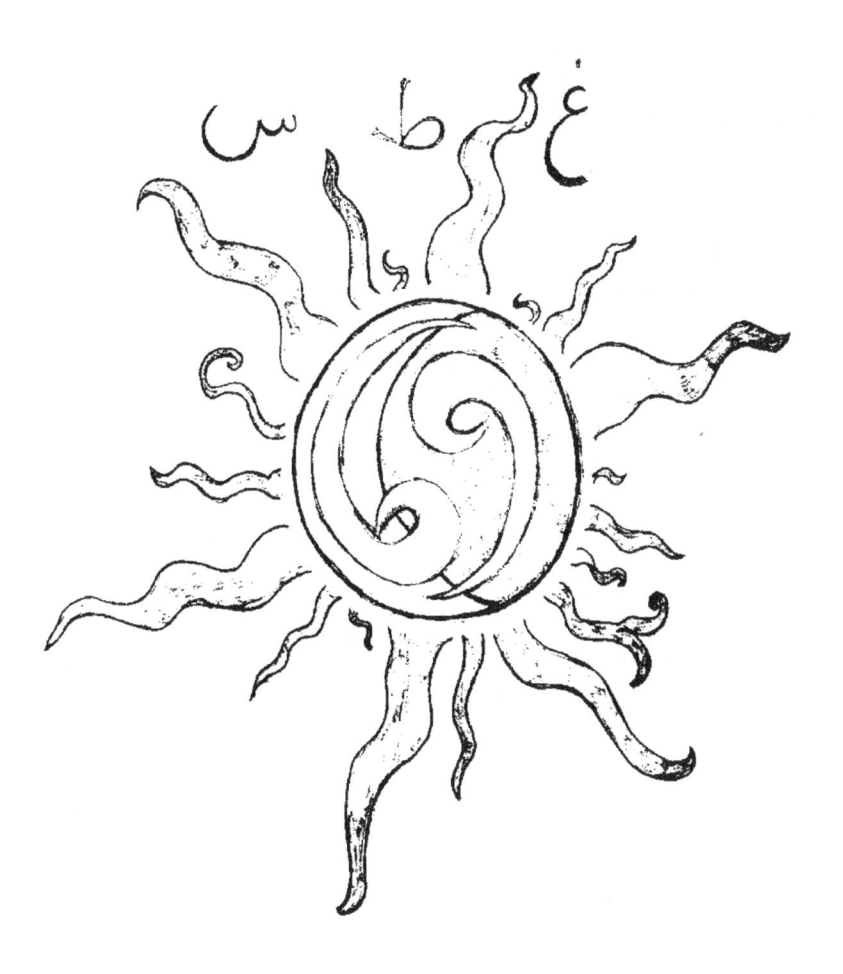

Unwritten Love

In a world full of passion,
self-determination and satisfaction.

There's an image of you and me,
but no description of what it means.

Yet a sense of security,
in its mesmerizing obscurity.

Alone

Alone,
> Bestowed upon me the darkness creeps.

No light to be seen,
> But the stars in the sky.

No one to be heard,
> But my footsteps in the night.

Alone,
> In the darkness I seek the truth.

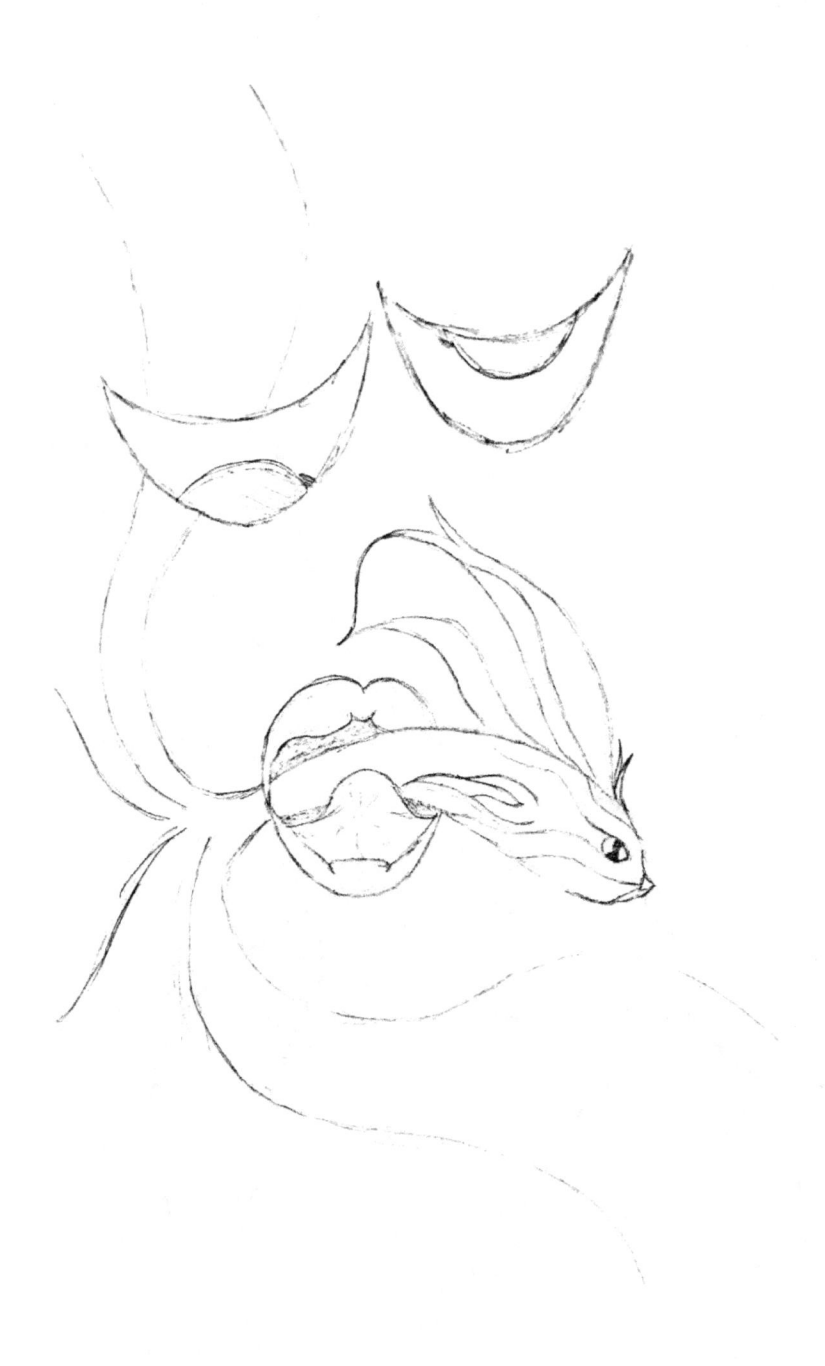

Nonsense

Too little days
Too many ways
Too little hi's
Too many bye's
Upside down or downside up?
Half-filled or half-empty cup?
Positives and negatives, opposites attract
Body over mind or mind over body?
Painting, knitting, which is hobby?
Heaven's sake or eternal glory?
Angry mob or floors of fury?

Pinky Promise

Too many things left unsaid
Too many things left undone

Forgive me for me
I forgive you for you

Fights will bring us closer
Kisses will make us lovers

Tell you everything cause you care
Tell you nothing cause you don't care
But you do, deep down inside
Because I know and so do you
And that's why I love you
Pinky promise I love you.

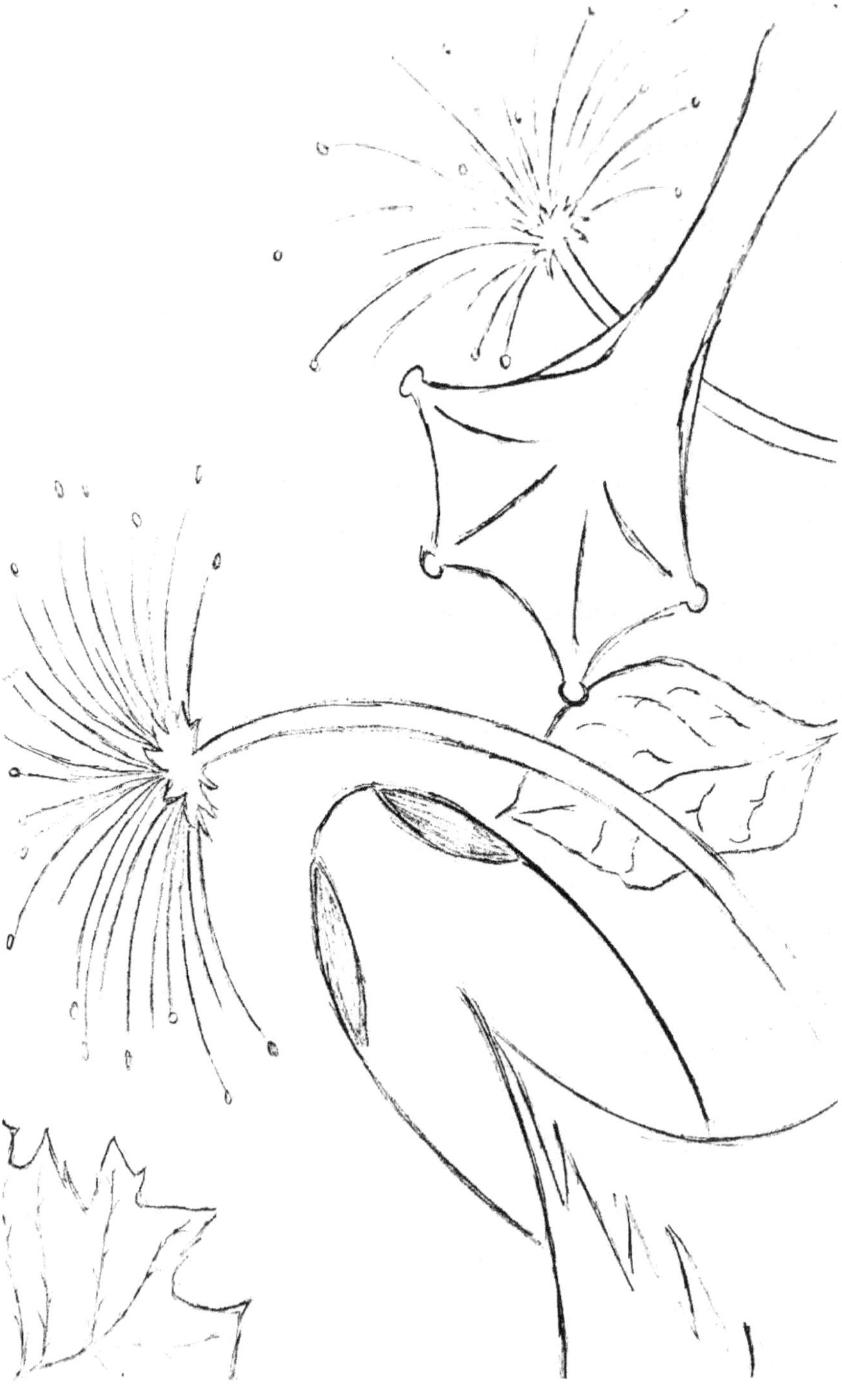

Smoke

Sweet and simple
Just enough, not too much
A puff in the sky
Not scattered, nor battered
A wisp and a whirl
With just one curl
Not twenty or thirty
Just one
That dangles lightly
Just one that shines brightly
Like being sun kissed
But maybe better
Something that was missed
That bump in the road
Life at the stoplight
And the midnight crow, crowed

Transfer of Pain

Life is cruel
Unusually painful
Whether it be through the state of mind
Or through physical abuse
My head throbs
Hold my breath
Maybe I'll get a taste of death
Green-blue veins
Raise through my skin
Pulse on its own high
All the tears blur my sight
Pound this fist against the wall
Hoping the anger is transferred
From my body to anything in sight
I want everything to feel my anger
My betrayal
My lost love

A Reason to Live

Life full of depression
Regret and repression

Is a life worth living for if everything you live for is gone?

How does one go on?
How does one act?

Somethings just shouldn't happen
Our minds too weak to contain the tragedies
Catastrophes, traumas, and experiences, not subtle for the human eye.

A Zephyr

Let the wind surround you
And wrap you in its arms.

The chills beneath your skin
Leave you oh so breathless.

So take this embracement
And close your eyes.

Howls of the Lone Wolf

Looking far and looking near,

The sun is setting,

The dark I fear.

Hesitation runs in my veins,

Danger lurking in and out,

Protect me, will you from these fangs?

The moon is out conducting magic,

Hear the howls of this beast,

Whose fate is oh so tragic.

His hair rises upon his back,

A trail of prints left in the dirt,

Flashlight low, silent, don't leave a track.

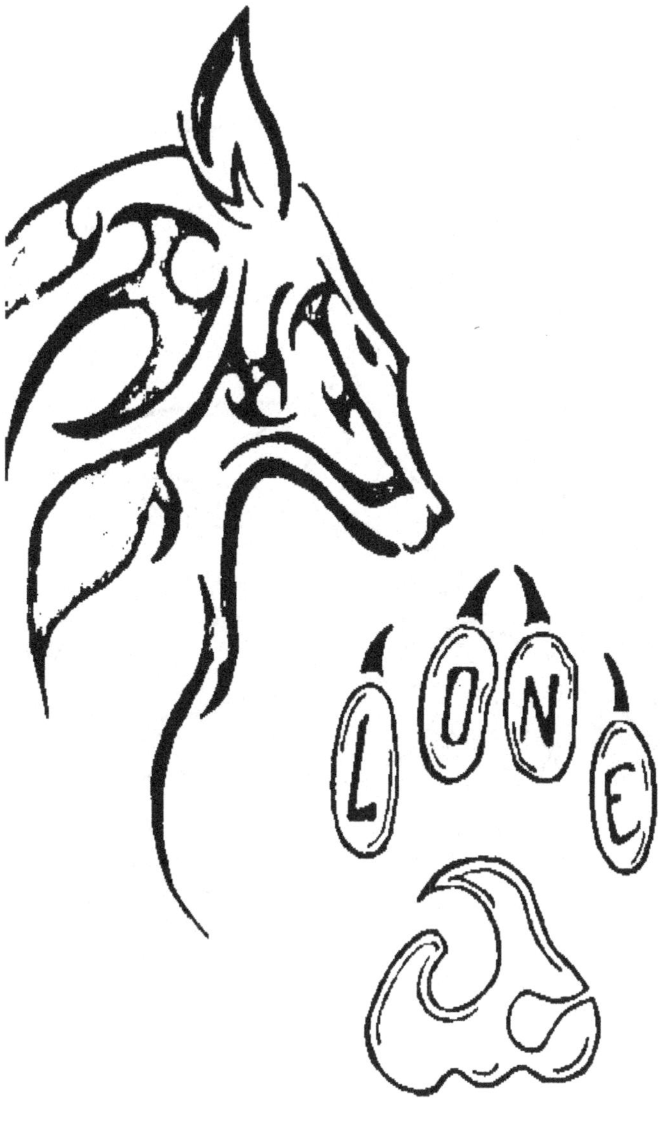
LONE

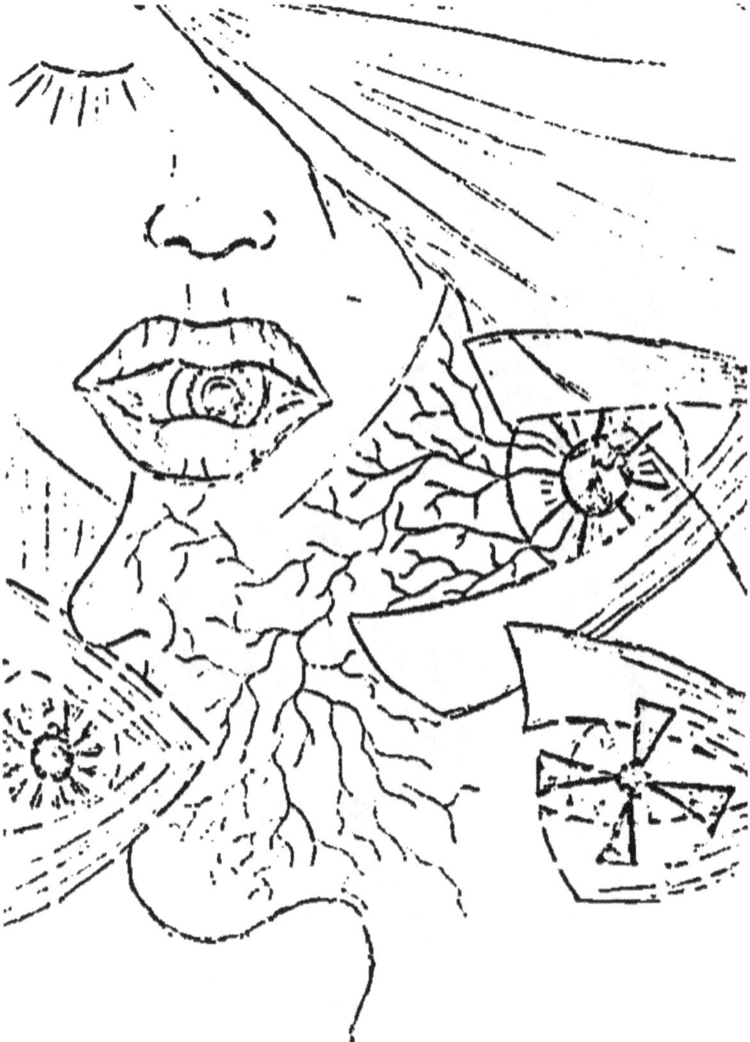

Eyes

There are so many eyes,
Those around me,
The ones that stare from above and down below me.

There are eyes in a distance, from afar,
Eyes near, they show no signs of fear.

The eyes are everywhere,
Even within me.

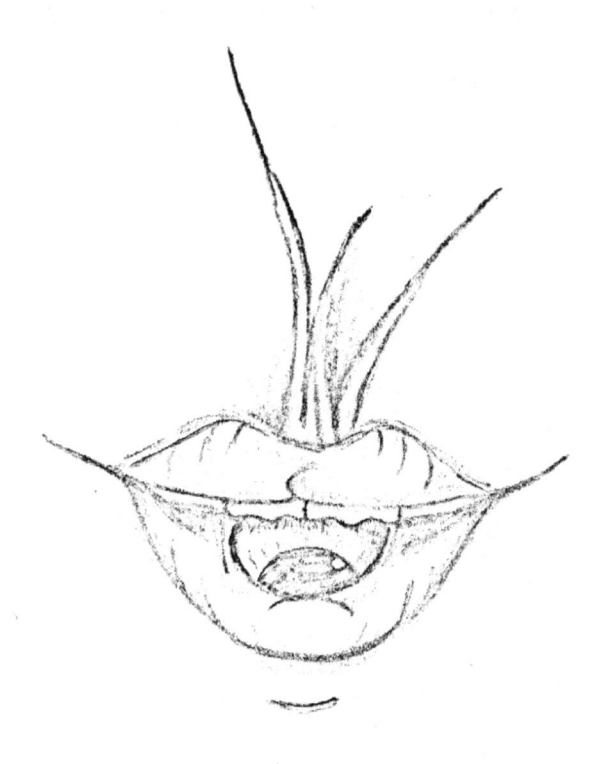

Dying Kiss

My mouth is raw and burning
A lack of oxygen in my lungs
Hold me close, my time has come
Kiss me sweetly,
Please once more.

Let yours be the last I have
Distract me from the pain that ripples through me
Orchestrate a love story with your words
Chest to chest,
Let your heart sing to me.

Actions

Another day of thoughts
we wish
we held.

Another day of words
we wish
we said.

To speak with dignity or act on instinct.
Will your words counteract your actions?

Dragon Scales and Fire Breath

New moons path shines bright on us
Misty fog over the ground
An eerie sense of death in the shadows.

His eyes glow green, his nostrils flare.
Moonlight shined bright upon the scales,
before the scorching red fire blazed upon the night.

Find Yourself

A face of happiness
Such a joke
A heart of sorrow
Filled with confusion.

Do not lead a life of lies
Find the truth within
Smiles will only cure so much
Your true path will set you free.

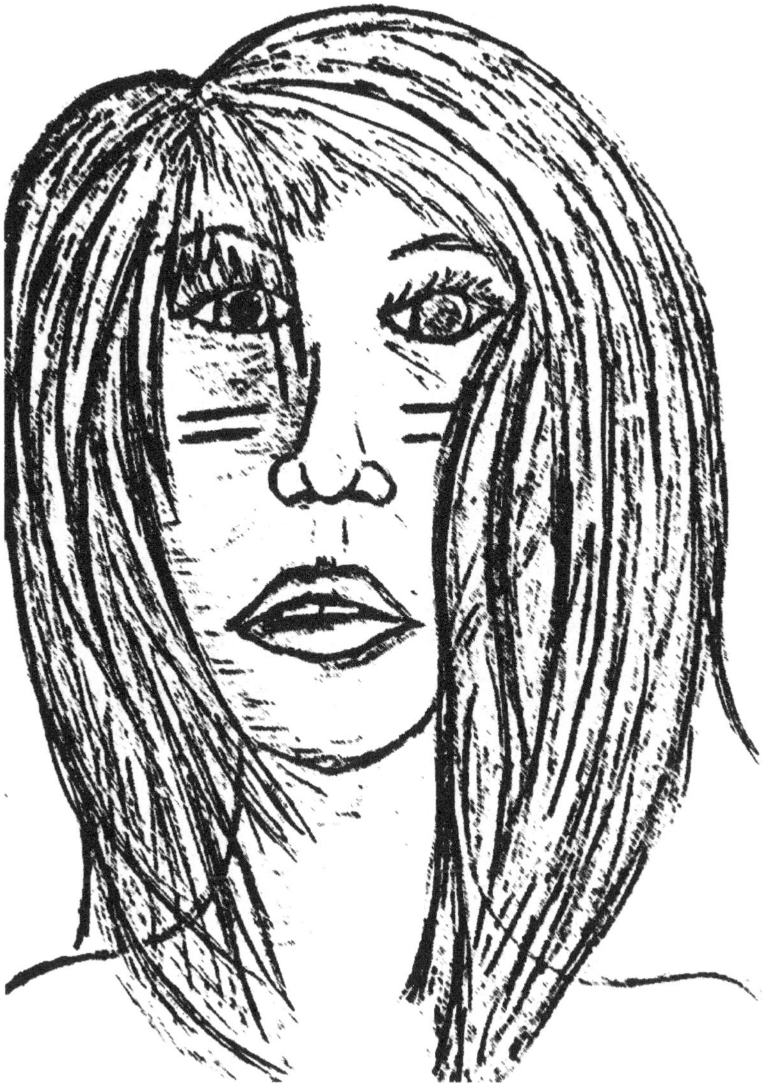

Alcoholic Reasons

I drink to ease the pain,

    so I don't have to cry myself to sleep.

Blacking out is a habit,

    so I don't have to remember your face.

Beauty of Words

I love the words.
That they write upon the blank sheet of paper.
As they flow into sentences.

Beautiful.

With meaning behind each word.
To each and every person.
No one's view is the same.
Perspective is amazing.
Each belonging to its owner.

What I read and what you read are not the same, yet it is, in a way.

So tell me.
Do you love words, the way I love words?

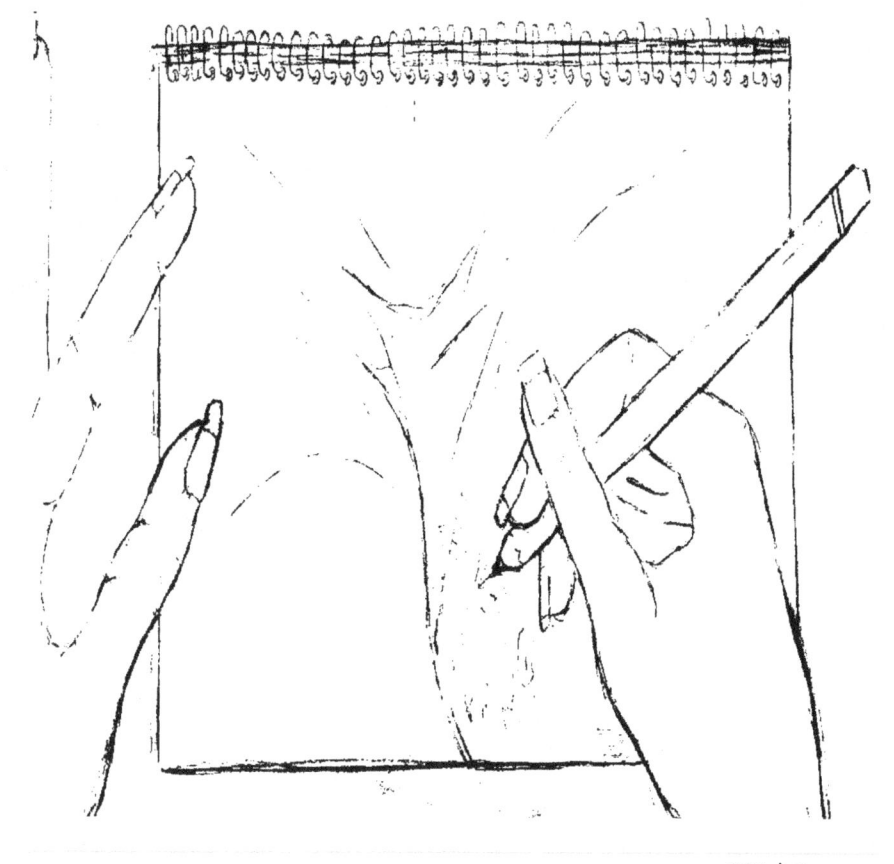

View

Sometimes we can't see the truth
And our minds are sent into oblivion
A state of incompleteness
Searching for something we already have
The truth was never to be found
Expand the mind and see
Open to different levels of recognition
Allow those ideas to flow in
Be open to this point of view

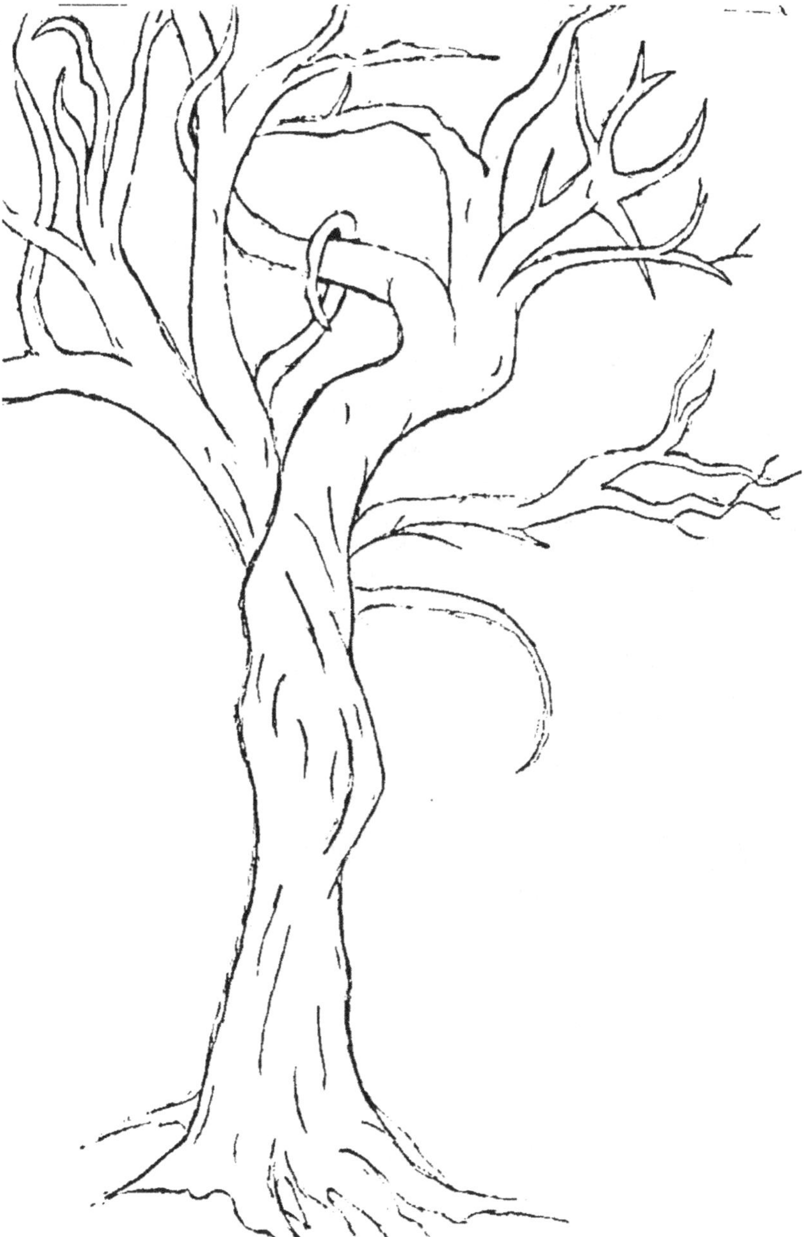

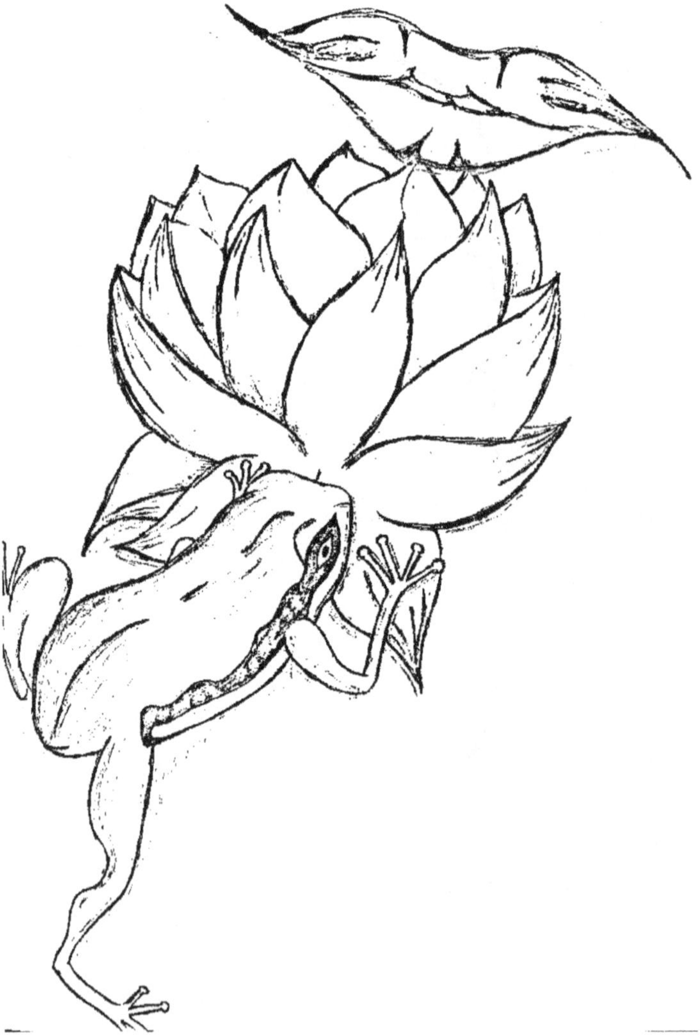

I Am Not Yours

These tears aren't for you,
These feelings I feel are not the feelings I feel for you.

Your bed is full of memories,
The ones I do not want with you.

Just leave me now and smile nice,
The lies I see right through your face.

Their Voices

And the voices filled the room in a harmonic way
One after another they spoke in twisted tongues
Languages of waters and of land, of fire, of air.

And once they started there was no escaping
This room, where words become the truth and reality.

S.A.D. and Company

Curiosity of innocent eyes,
In a world with unforgiving obstacles.

Learning to overcome, to survive,
Takes more than a pretty smile.

The courage, strength, and support,
To not only survive, but to thrive.

In a world where they knock you down for your differences,
Their ignorance is not our bliss.

It's like a curse that can't be broken,
Until we realize that we don't need to meet their standards.

We are different,
And we are proud.

I Wonder

I wonder what the world would be like,

If it never changed.

Would all the people be the same?

Cookie cutter in design?

Trust

Trust your instincts.

Believe in yourself, in your choices.

Be your own advocate when no one else will.

Self-will and self-preservation.

Push forward and never back down.

Their negativity and selfishness will not affect you.

Stay strong.

Move on.

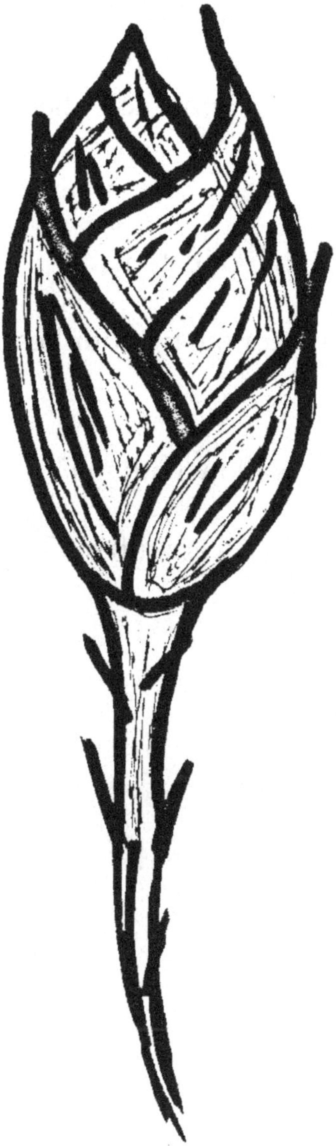

Me Too

Does a smile stretch across your face when you think of me?

Do butterflies erupt?

Taking flight in the pit of your stomach?

Does the love you have for me fill your heart and run through your veins?

When I'm sad, do you wallow with me?

When I'm happy, do you cheer with me?

If you answered yes,

    I just want to say,

        me too.

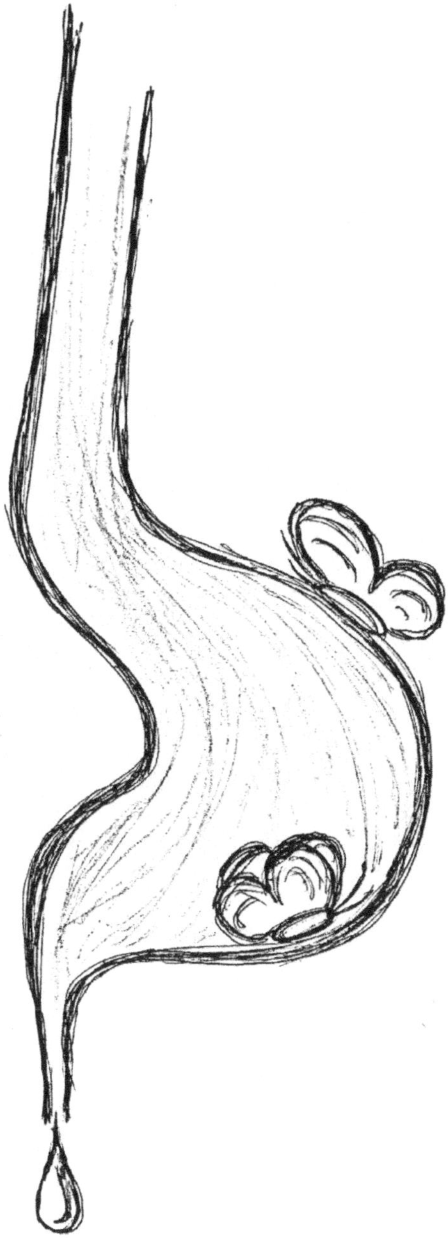

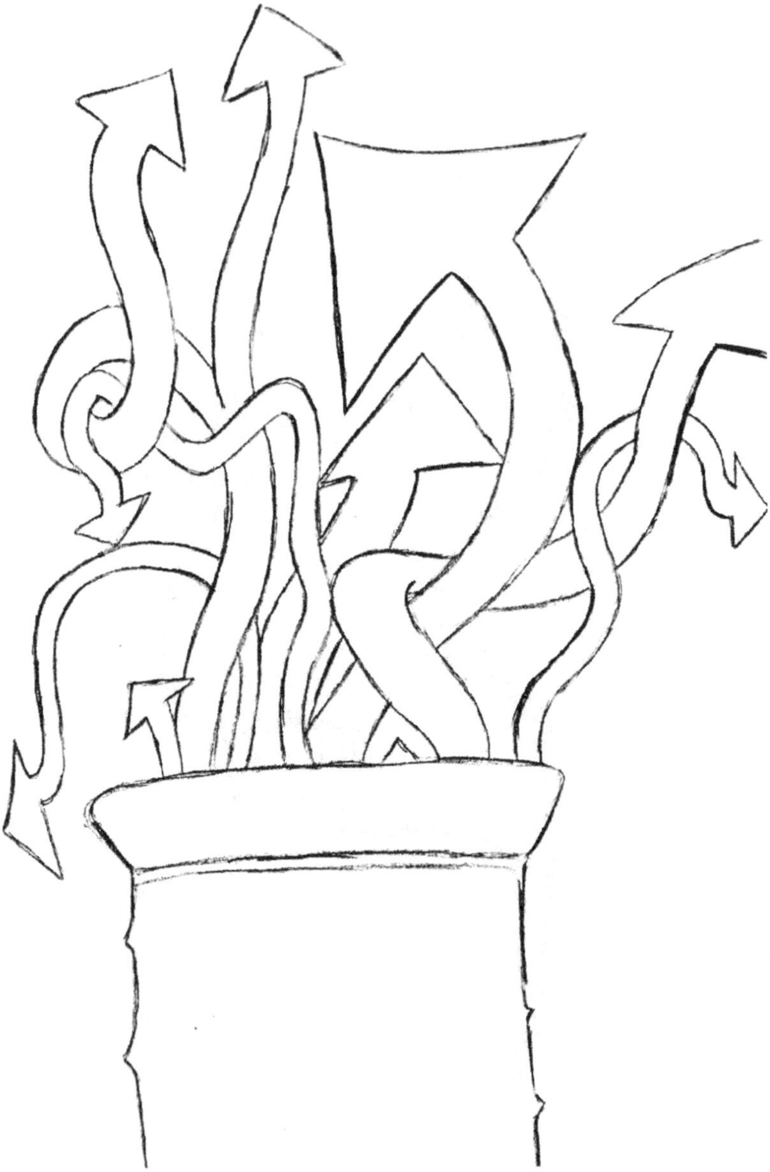

Pit of my Stomach

I feel the sickness in the pit of my stomach.

A violent prick against my core.

Make it stop.

I beg of you.

The nauseating tension,

I can't take it.

I lay in bed and try to sleep.

But all I see is you,

As you haunt my dreams.

Everyday

Every day you amaze me.

Every day I see your face and I smile

Every day I pray I don't go a day without you.

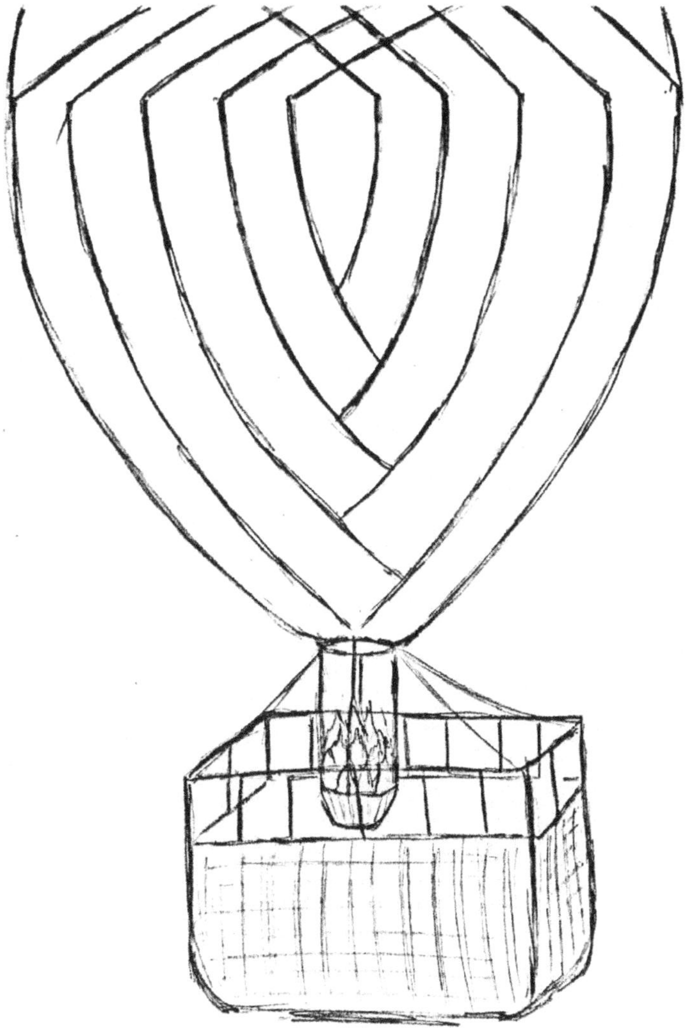

Suicide

How difficult is it,

to resist the urge,

to end your own life,

when it seems,

you have nothing,

left to live for?

The Grin Reaper

You can see a fake smile from a mile away.

The grin is not real.

You can tell at the corner of pursed lips.

The way they slyly fold upwards.

A smile be cautious to trust.

Not every smile, is a friend.

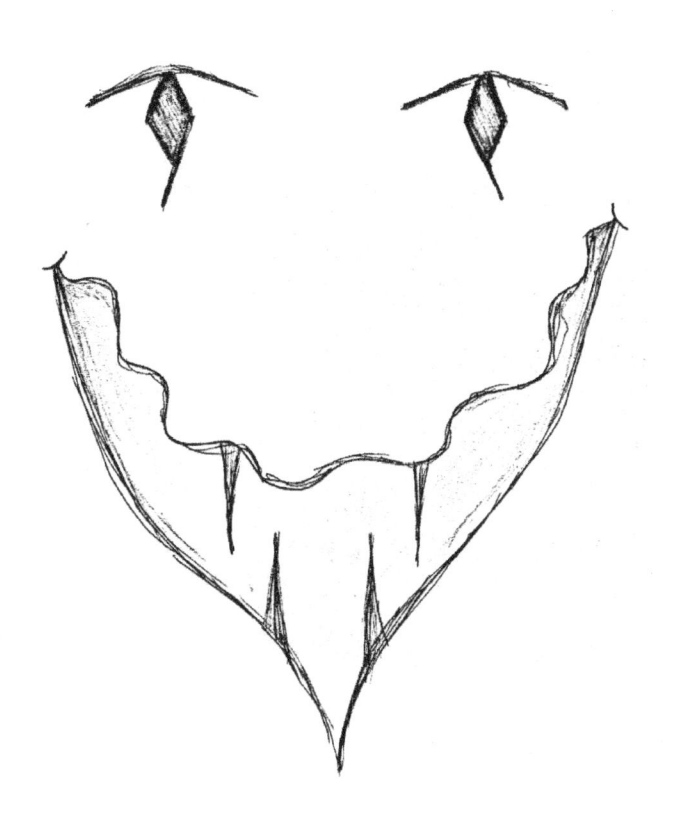

I Am My Own Motivation

I am funny

I am loved

I am somebody

I am important

I can do this

I am beautiful

I can do anything

I am smart

I am strong

I am not weak

I am worth it

I am strong

I am worthy

I don't need him

I am special

I don't need him

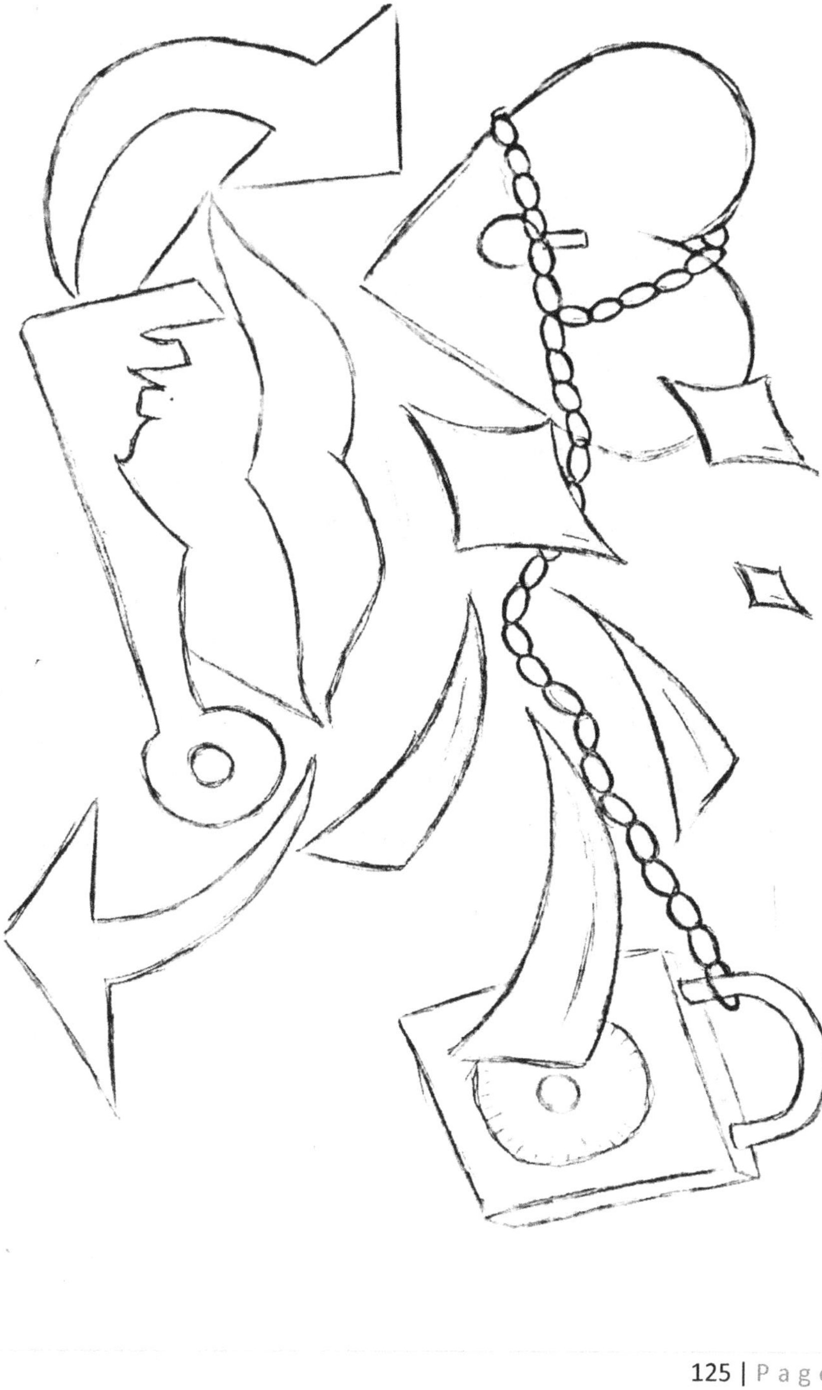

Desire

Desire,

To be irresistibly desirable,

To lay in the arms of a man and feel complete.

To know that his eyes do not stray,

That you have his full and undivided attention.

Isn't that what we crave?

What we crave to have and experience?

To have that.

To be loved.

To be wanted.

To be desired.

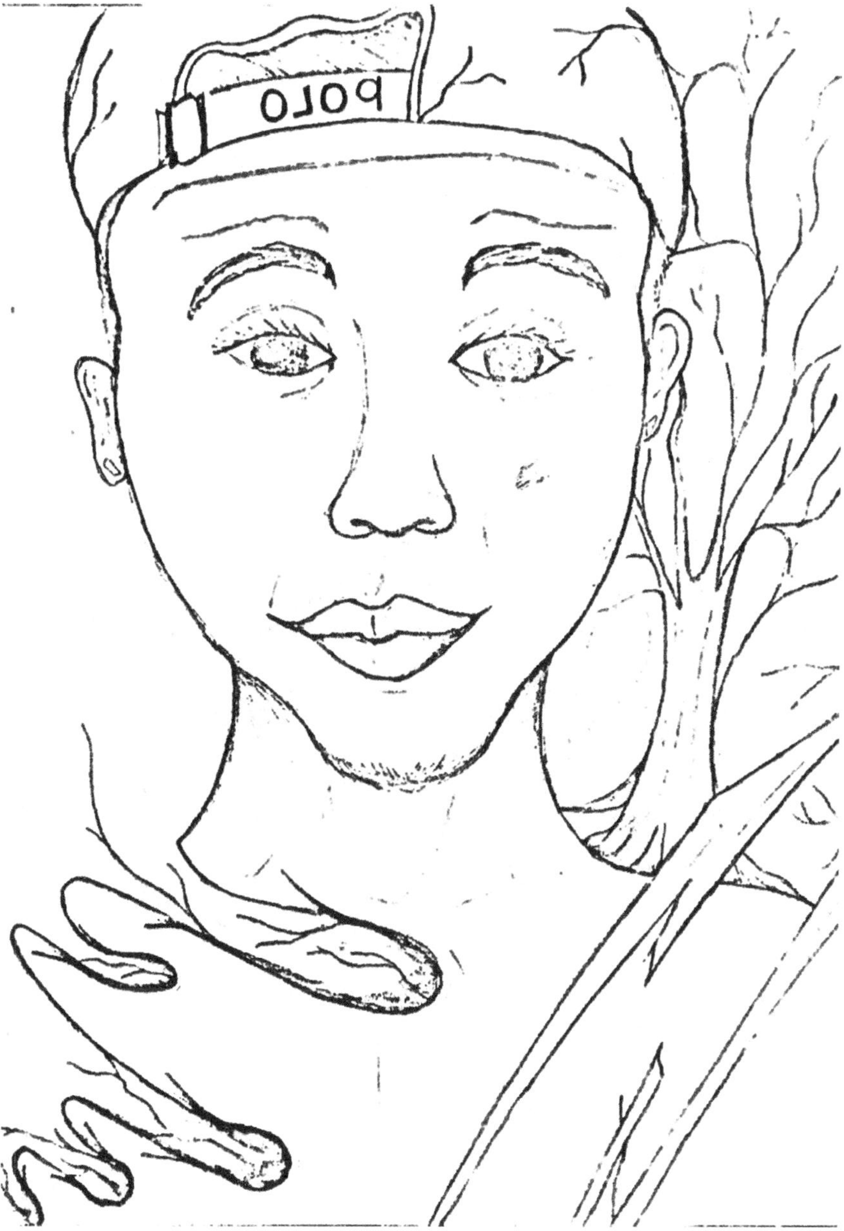

Taylor
A short story

    A simple girl, full of the innocence they threw upon her. Her hair lay twisted in a pony tail on the top of her head. Her sun battered skin appeared painted, splattered with two toned spots. She looked at herself in the mirror, dark brown eyes stared back at her. Sincerely thinking that if she stared long enough the dark blue lining of her eyes would enclose and the blue eyes she was born with would return. But logically they wouldn't. Shrugging off the thought she pushed play on the iPod and applied the black eyeliner that enhanced her eyes. Grabbing her bag and keys she headed out the door and started the car.

    Driving down the unfamiliar street she approached the neighborhood call box and punched in the appropriate numbers. Pulling up to the last house, she put the car in park, moved over to the passenger seat and waited. Catching a glimpse of him from the rear-view mirror, she picked up her book and began to read. He came up to the car and knocked on the window. She unlocked the door, and he let himself in. He took the keys she handed him, and they drove off.

    He plugged in his iPod and let the music flow through the car to lighten the mood. "What are you reading?" She looked into his ocean blue eyes and said, "If you were my man," and turned back to continue her novel.

He Saved Her
A short story

Her face held the truth. It was so easy to read her. The innocence that was once there, now replaced. The deepness beneath her eyes revealed many sleepless nights. Maybe she cried herself to sleep. Or maybe she had nightmares that awoke her in a sweat. Looking too long at the phone, waiting for a message, a call, anything. Waiting for nothing… those questions arose, and they asked themselves as they walked past her. Never directly would they approach her. Just looking into her eyes was all they had to do. They told her story. They told them exactly what they wanted to hear. Her lips barely moved. They just sat there upon her face. Still. If it weren't for the pinkish shade that filled them they might have come off lifeless.

Set deep in the misery that she carried with her. All she wanted was what everyone wants out of life. But things weren't looking too bright. More than usual the darkness followed in her footsteps. It scared her more than ever. She didn't want to think about the things that ran through her head. The images that haunted her dreams that came in the night. They illuminated the light at the end of the tunnel, always leaving her with questions. Pain seemed to be the only release.

No one listened. No one cared. No one even knew. It killed her that she had no one. Slowly and inevitably it would surly get to her. Little by little she began making up excuses for the bruises on her hand. Her pinky was swollen and could hardly move. It was an accident she would say. But if you looked at the mahogany desk that was placed in the corner of her room, you would catch a glimpse of indentions.

But no one saw. And no one persistently asked. They just nodded their heads and gave her ice and smiled.

Accusations and assumptions, they were like vultures. They covered her every move, waiting for her to slip up. Why now? Before she was no one, and now she was the focal point of pure jealousy. She had gone to desperate lengths to feel wanted. To feel desired. To be desired. To be wanted. If she was or not was a question that may never be answered. But the feeling was always with her while he was around.

And so, she stuck to him, even if it turned on her in the end. Leaving her right where she had started alone, desperate, and hurting. Guilt consumed her. So, she inhaled. Inhaled and exhaled, letting it enter her bloodstream. The effects were pleasurable and excused her of her misery till she woke up the following morning. Again, and again she would lie and leave the house. She always returned with Christmas eyes and the thirst of a man in the desert. And when the thirst got too bad, she would drown it, quenching at the taste.

Regardless of the burn she continued. Sip after sip till reality had become a faint faded memory that she had no care for. But that was the problem, she cared too much. It was something within her. It was something that she had been born with. Did she ask for this? Did she ask for the need to help and love others? No. It was just her nature. But this nature had turned on her and only made her weaker. She couldn't shake it off. It was an everlasting contract between her and sensitivity.

She had wanted nothing more but to let go for a while. She wanted to be emotionless, to shut off her humanity even.

She leaned towards those who were like her. One in particular, had mastered the effect of shutting off all emotions. But that had left him mean. In public it was like he had no care in to the world but when he got home the only way he could keep himself from not crying was to just sleep. And sleep his life away. He slept until the dreams had taken over and he was exactly where he wanted to be. He was finally surrounded by love.

Getting close to him was a mistake, but she did it anyways. She desired his presence but was afraid her need for him would drive him away. But he understood her and was there for her when she needed him. Starlight nights consumed them. Entering a world where no one saw them, and they were free to do as they pleased. No one could take away the satisfaction they got from one another's presence.

He taught her how to hold it in, how to completely turn into someone who was as unemotional as a rock on the side of the road. Or the stone-cold face of a pebble that skipped into the water. Never to be skipped again because the blue hands dragged it in too deep. He taught her control, and to smile.

Even when times got hard, as they always did, he taught her to smile in the face of defeat. Smile in the face of horror. Smile in the face of those who have no faith in you and just want to see you fail. It brought her peace. To see those who hated her squirm when she didn't react as they thought she would when they approached her.

She was still sad. But she wasn't when she was with him. He knew the consequences. He knew that he couldn't help her hold back everything. And she didn't want to. She wanted to share what she was feeling with him. And that scared him. It would send him through a whirl wind of undesired feelings that he locked up. Uncovering them would make him vulnerable. She was willing to be so, but he wasn't.

Tattered, beaten, thrown, and left in sorrow. He wasn't ready to go back to that place in where he would completely let someone in, and he wasn't going to mistakenly let her make her way in either. He gave her reasons and options. She weighed them and understood, to the point where she could have ruined everything she was working so hard to keep pure. If it wasn't for that one thing, that one simple question. Are you sure?

Abandoned
A short story

    I was a boy, merely at the age of five and I was left at the steps that led into the catholic church. My parents told me I was going to mass alone while they went shopping. I was five, gullible and naïve. But isn't that any five-year-old? Abandonment. I was alone and scared as I waited for the twin stained glass doors to open and let me in. But they never did. Yet I sat and waited anyways. I didn't want to upset my parents, so I waited. Reaching into my backpack I grabbed a juice box and some crackers. My mother packed these for the church, she said they were to be donated. But I was starving, and the sun was setting. I had nothing with me except that bag of food and the clothes on my back.

    The street lights started coming on and the sunset was slowly fading into the distant horizon. I was five years old, and I was left on the steps of the neighborhood church. Nobody came for me, nobody called my name to see if I was okay, or if I wanted something to eat. I laid my head on top of my backpack and shut my eyes praying that when I woke up I'd be in my mother's arms in the safety of my home.

The City of the Rich
A short story

I was in a city where there were two types of people. The socially accepted rich, and the looked down upon poor. In this city, I was considered poor. I dressed in dirty jeans and a bland rag-like top. My hair was long and coiled in a messy bun. The poor walked the streets during the day searching for food that the rich threw away and scraps of materials we could use to make our insufficient shacks more suitable for living. The meaning of life of the poor here was to kneel to the rich and to fear them. Our lives were merely for the entertainment of those who had money to spare for days. Everyday walking the streets you'd see a body or two just laid out on the street with mournful faces, their palms faced upwards as if waiting for that one slice of soggy bread that could have kept them breathing another day.

Life here was miserable, especially when the tornados came. They spread open like the mouth of a beast consuming everything but the houses of the rich. Nothing they owned could be harmed by the tornados. They knew how to protect themselves. Yet once in a while you would hear about that one drunken rich guy that got sucked up trying to look tough up against the monstrous gray cloud of air and wind. The city people would mourn over his sacred life, but never acknowledged us. Only to insult us and mock us of our pathetic lives. I hated them, I hated them with a passion so deep that I could feel the blood boiling in my body.

Walking along the streets of the rich, I kept my head low as I tried to find dinner for my family. The road hurt my bare feet but still I went on. Then the siren went off. The siren to warn you to stay indoors, or in my case to get underground. But I was nowhere near home and not even a foolish rich person would let me into their safe haven. Looking off into the horizon I saw it. The cloudy whirl winds that would end my life. I didn't even get to reach nineteen. I heard a scream close by to me, my head turned quickly to see a child. He stood in the middle of the street hollering for his parents. The wind began to get stronger as the tornado moved in. The little boy was rich, I could tell how his blonde hair stuck to his head combed back with a glossy shine. I didn't see anybody looking for him, so I ran to him. He screamed as tears ran down his rosy cheeks, "Momma! Papa!"

    The wind started pulling me back, and without much thought I grabbed the boy as I started to lift from the ground. Just as I was about to be taken up into the dark sky I saw a lamppost and reached out my hand. Getting a hold of it I brought my legs around it and kept the crying boy close to me. His flimsy arms wrapped around my waste as he buried his wet face into my rag top. The darkness got closer, fiercely trying to rip me and the boy off the lamppost. With all the strength in me I held on, I wouldn't let go. I screamed. There was no light around us. The wind undid my hair as it began it to unleash itself in the fury. The tornado was passing right over us. slowly the winds died down. The streets began to clear up. Debris filled the streets as leaves floated down from above.

    Shaken, I peeled my rigid hands and legs from the post. I tried to set the boy down, but he scrambled up me and wrapped his arms around my neck and his legs around my waist. I was shocked, I had never been so close to someone rich.

"Hey, are you okay?" I asked gently. I felt the boy nod yes, but he wouldn't let go. "Where do you live?" I had to get him home before his parents had my head for dinner. He let one scrawny arm off of my neck and turned his head facing me. He looked at me with a deep set of baby blue eyes as if to say thank you. Using his index finger, he pointed the way toward his house, or should I say mansion.

The child lived in one of the biggest houses on the block. I tried to let him down when we got to the side walk of his house, but still the child wouldn't budge. He continued to point forward, I had never stepped onto a property of the rich. It was like a death sentence. Yet I went on, I stopped at the doorstep and tried again to set him down again. Nothing. He only hung to me tighter. I gulped as I raised my fist to knock on the door. Faintly I could hear the screams of a woman crying. I stepped back and waited. The door swung open as a woman about my height answered the door. Her face was caked with make-up, and a floral printed dress covered her body. The long blonde curly hair and blue eyes she had resembled that of the boys. Her eyes widened as she saw the boy, "Herald he's here, he's alive!"

She was hysterical as she reached for the boy not even giving me notice. The boy slowly unraveled himself from me as his mother held him in her arms. A man came running down the white dipped stairs, the boy's father I presumed. We made eye contact and I saw a look of disgust. I turned around and began to leave. "No! Wait!" the voice of the little boy called out for me.

I turned around and looked as he pushed himself away from his parents and ran over to me. Taking hold of my hand as he walked back toward the house. He smiled up at me with dirt smudges on his face. The look on his parents faces had me scared, what would they do with me? His mother crossed her arms and said, "Now come in and join us for dinner, would you?"

It almost knocked me over to hear those words leave her mouth. "You - you want me to ha - have dinner with you?" The man let out an old man's chuckle as he replied, "Well of course we do, you saved our son Benjamin's life, didn't you? We are eternally grateful." As he said this he removed his hat and bowed to me. I was about to pass out. There has never been such an occurrence of a rich man bowing down to a dirty poor girl. Hesitantly, I walked into the house. The tiles were cold to my bare feet. "Leo! Leo Honey, come down please!" The woman called out. A few seconds later a young man came waking down the stairs. He had pitch black hair and mesmerizing green eyes. His face was gorgeous, I've never seen anyone so perfect. "Yes mother?" he questioned as he saw me.

"Can you please take -- Well where are my manners? I'm sorry dear I didn't get your name."

"My name is Souli." I said.
"Well Souli, its truly a pleasure, I am Anisa, this is my husband Herald, my son Leo, and I assume you know little Benjamin."
"It's very nice to meet you all." I said lowering my head a little.

"Now Leo please show our guest to the wash room and fetch her something to change into, she will be joining us for dinner." A surprised look was on his face as he heard his mother, but he did as she said. He held out his arm for me, so I slowly wrapped my hand around his arm. He smiled at me and lead me up the stairs. When we got to the top of the stairs he guided me to a room that was covered in beautiful white tiles, everything sparkled with cleanliness. I stood in the washroom taking everything in, Leo handed me a towel and fresh clothes to change into.

"Enjoy," he said as started for the door.
"Wait.." I called out. Embarrassed of what I was about to say, "I don't know how to turn that on." Looking at the shower he walked over and showed me how to turn the knob to get the water started, left and I would get cold water, right and I would get hot water. "Thank you," I said as I looked up at him.
"No problem." He said as he shut the door behind him.

I turned the knob to the right, I removed my rags and folded them on the side table. Stepping into the shower I was amazed at the way the water felt. It was so warm, and it flowed evenly down my body. The bottom of the shower turned a murky brown from the dirt that lingered. I had never felt so pampered. To be invited into the house of the rich was unheard of in my side of the city. And here I was lathering myself with their rich soap in their rich shower. I closed my eyes and stood there thinking.
When I opened my eyes, it was gone. "No," I whispered. I had fallen asleep in a field of flowers. This was all a dream.

Follow Solaine T. Gerhard

Website: www.Solainetgerhard.com
Facebook: www.Facebook.com/solainetgerhard
Instagram: Solainetgerhard

About the Author

Solaine Gerhard is an American-Brazilian writer who grew up in Lake Worth, Florida with her parents and younger sister. As Robert James Waller once said, "Life is never easy for those who dream." Gerhard fully believes in this saying, which is shown through her writings. She finds inspiration in all aspects of her life, helping to guide her creative style of expression.

In Gerhard's senior year at Lake Worth High School, she performed as Lady in Orange in the play *For Colored Girls Who Have Considered Suicide / When the Rainbow is Enuf*. In the same year, 2012 she was inducted into the Thespian Honor Society. In 2016 she received her Bachelor of Science in biology from Florida Gulf Coast University. Gerhard is currently working towards her second bachelor's degree in nursing at Rasmussen College.

Made in United States
Orlando, FL
28 March 2024